P.E. 85/6

ACCIDENTS HAPPEN

Why do light aeroplane pilots fly into clouds stuffed with mountains? What causes balloonists to sever high-voltage power cables? How has a yachtsman had his bowsprit run over by a train? According to Ann Welch errors such as these – sometimes resulting in fatalities – cannot be attributed only to carelessness, misapprehension or poor memory; the reason lies deeper. At a time when opportunities for involvement in sports such as diving, flying, mountaineering and sailing are at their greatest, we risk becoming less capable of doing them safely or competently through lack of practice in being responsible for ourselves.

The problems of confusions and mistakes which can arise in leisure activities using sophisticated equipment, such as gliders or scuba gear, are examined. The author goes on to discuss many related aspects ranging from the effects of poor equipment design in light aeroplanes to the disorientating consequences of alien environments, for example being trapped under water or lost in fog. As a sailor, a highly qualified aeroplane pilot and experienced gliding instructor, Ann Welch lays particular emphasis on the role of the instructor as a maker of safety or potential disaster, and on the importance of clear communication.

Numerous true stories – some ludicrous, others hair-raising – illustrate not only what sort of predicaments ordinary, sensible human beings can so easily become involved in, but *how* such situations develop and how people can overcome them.

ACCIDENTS HAPPEN is essential reading for all those concerned with safety in sport and is absorbing to read because of the realisation that 'There but for the grace of God go I.'

D1615116

ALSO BY ANN WELCH
Pilots' Weather

WITH LORNE WELCH
The Story of Gliding

WITH LORNE WELCH & FRANK IRVING
New Soaring Pilot

ACCIDENTS HAPPEN

Anticipation · Avoidance · Survival

✧ Ann Welch

DRAWINGS BY PIERS BOIS

JOHN MURRAY

My son shall learn to sail a boat before he drives a car. In a sailboat he gets power only through his discipline and his ability to meet and master nature. But in the motor car he gets power without discipline and without control.

JOSIAH ROYCE

Printed in Great Britain by
Cox & Wyman Ltd,
London, Fakenham and Reading
0 7195 3545 X (cased)
0 7195 3552 2 (paperback)

◇ CONTENTS

Part Four: After the Dust Settles

✧ INTRODUCTION

It is quite difficult to invent a new accident; almost every possible confusion has already occurred – a submarine has collided with a cyclist, an aeroplane towing a glider has taken off without a pilot in either aircraft, and a yachtsman has had his bowsprit run over by a train. There is nothing surprising in this because all of us make mistakes most of the time and there are a lot of people in the world all hard at it. Accidents are part of the constant trial-and-error process of living and they result from the fumbles that start with the intrinsic experiments of childhood and continue right through to the forgetfulness or confusion of old age. Along the way the possibilities for disaster are considerable.

Since a book about accidents in general would be endless, these pages are limited largely to the perils and problems arising from such activities as flying, sailing or sub-aqua diving where, in addition to human follies and foibles, there is the often complex operation of sophisticated equipment. In or under the water, on high mountains, or in the air the human not only has to try to avoid making his usual run of everyday mistakes and use his equipment properly, but is also in a hostile environment. He cannot just stop by the roadside and take a breather. He has to sort out any problems which occur, or which he creates, for himself. Although all these activities are fun and give enormous pleasure, they also impose a harsh discipline which for most of the time may not be apparent. They charge a high price for just the same sort of mistake as forgetting to post a letter, running the car too low on petrol, or putting tea in the coffee pot. Life suddenly changes from one in which small errors are mostly not important into one where they can be vital.

The problem is that most of us live in a regulated and protected world. If something is lost it can be replaced, and is frequently paid for by insurance. If we are ill, even through our own fault, a vast system exists for repairing the damage. Food is available pre-washed, frozen or canned; warmth and water is on tap. Street corners have guardrails to stop us from walking under a car and beach-guards prevent us carelessly drowning ourselves. If we fall over the cliff the vigilant coastguard will pull us up again. If we drift out to sea on a li-lo the R.N.L.I. will fetch us back to the friendly land. All this is very nice and convenient, but it has resulted in a fairly massive loss of those qualities of self-reliance, even of individual responsibility; we have become citizens of the Dependent Society. At a time when the opportunities for involving ourselves in things like flying, diving, sailing and mountaineering are probably at their greatest, we risk becoming less capable of doing them either safely or even competently, because we have become out of practice in being responsible for ourselves. We fail to appreciate that everything that is provided, whether it be a supermarket, regulations and licences, or packaged courses of instruction take something away from our ability to select, or to take decisions; for making up our own minds and working things out – for ourselves. It is easy for the pilot with a valid medical certificate to feel that it is no longer necessary for him to decide for himself whether he is actually fit to fly, and natural for a person completing a dinghy sailing course to feel that he is now 'qualified' when in fact he has been taught only pre-selected aspects of boat operation.

Living in a dependent society offers little incentive either to want, or be forced, to do anything properly. There is no need to preserve food carefully in the summer to avoid starving in the winter. There is no need to become highly skilled at work because there is the dole. It is only, and it may seem surprising, in the so-called recreational activities, like flying hang gliders or diving, that it becomes apparent that here is something which it is essential to do properly; because the price of failure could be our own neck.

Mistakes and accidents, because they are such a fundamental part of life are sometimes very funny; the discomfiture of others raises great hilarity – the banana skin syndrome. But they may also be expensive, time-wasting and tragic. Obviously, it is desirable that accidents should as far as possible be avoided, at least the inept and unnecessary ones. However, they will never cease, and attempts to prevent them by warnings or regulations are sometimes counter-productive. Over-regulation can produce not only genuine failure to know what the rules are, but reaction against them. Basic rules, such as stopping at red traffic lights, are obviously sensible, are obeyed, and create a safer situation. With over-regulation, as with over-protection, particularly when it also adds to the operating costs, safety declines. Accidents will occur less frequently only if we understand what causes them, particularly those produced by our own human errors, and if responsibility for our actions – and the result of these actions – is carried firmly on our own shoulders. There is no question of turning the clock back; aids, organisation, and services are likely to increase, rather than go away; we need to appreciate that in the ultimate no one is concerned with our neck except ourselves. We need to go about things on the basis that no one will be around to help overcome our problems or dash to the rescue. We need to bring a little nearer the surface those fast disappearing instincts for survival. Having an accident is not really anything to be pleased about, and certainly most of us feel our feathers thoroughly ruffled if we make a nonsense of something. It is easy to blame others, but usually the fault is our own, so we are in the best position to learn from whatever folly it is we have perpetrated – if granted the opportunity.

All the stories in this book are true but it may seem that most involve flying or sailing. This is not because these two activities have the most accidents but because those that do

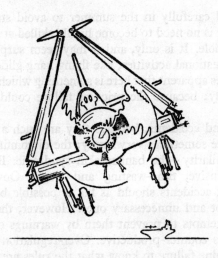

occur are in general well documented and because the variety of errors that can be made is wide ranging. But it is only the technology that is a bit different from other sports, such as diving, parachuting, mountaineering, or ballooning: the mistakes are the same.

The stories and information in this book have been drawn from many sources, and the most valuable have been the published first-hand accounts of mistakes and confusions written honestly by the victims themselves. My grateful thanks are due to them and to the editors and publishers of the many magazines and handbooks who obviously believe in a practical, common-sense approach to safety, including: *Aerostat, AOPA Pilot, Australian Safety Digest, Climber and Rambler, Coastguard, Flight International, Flight Safety Bulletin, Hang Gliding,* HMSO safety publications, *Lifeboat,* Ogwen Valley Mountain Rescue first-aid publications, *Pilot, Pilot Privé, Practical Boat Owner, Sail, Sailplane and Gliding, Skin Diver, Soaring, Sport Parachutist, Triton, Yachting Monthly, Yachting World, Wings!*

I would also like to thank the following for their great co-operation and help: the Rescue Services of the Royal Navy and the Royal Air Force, H.M. Coastguard, R.N.L.I. Sail Training Association and Fort Bovisand Underwater Centre.

PART ONE

◇ *Being Human is Trouble*

1 ◇ 'PILOT ERROR'

In the early days of flying the machines often went wrong, or fell apart, and such failures caused, and were rightly blamed for, most accidents. As aeroplanes improved and became more reliable accidents were blamed increasingly on 'pilot error'. This term persisted and was a simple way of allocating blame; if the aircraft was not found to be at fault, then the pilot must be – and often was. But 'pilot error' is neither a simple nor a single cause. It is many different causes conveniently lumped together, facets of human character which produce different actions or reactions, with all manner of fascinating confusions along the way. Pilot error includes forgetfulness, carelessness, unawareness or no understanding of the problem, irresponsibility, procrastination, pride, ignorance and straightforward incompetence. In a broad sense it implies that the individual was supposed to know enough to have appreciated that what he was doing was erroneous, and to have some understanding of the risks involved.

Poor Memory

At the top of the list of everyday errors and failings is forgetfulness or poor memory. The reason, too, is simple. There is just too much to have to remember. If one considers the amount of information – input and output, that most people cope with each day – much of it trivial or irrelevant, it is surprising that the average memory copes as well as it does. Support for this over-burdened twentieth-century faculty is given at every turn, provided by dictionaries, telephone directories, yellow pages, address books, diaries, conversion tables, shopping lists, time signals and bank statements. But there is still too much that has to be remembered, not least of which are second-order requirements, such as where the shopping list was left. In general forgetting something is inconvenient rather than critical, and most people learn to live with their indifferent memories without too much of a problem. But flying is unforgiving of forgetfulness, which is why formal pre-flight check-lists have become essential. Most light aeroplanes are quite complex devices in which flaps, power settings, fuel tank selection, pumps, beacons and brakes – air and wheel – all have to be operated correctly, otherwise the flight is inclined to be short on success. Nevertheless, in spite of having a check-list, and having been taught from the beginning to use it, some pilots still forget to carry it out at all, or completely. Recently no less than two pilots took off and flew to another airfield with concrete tie-down blocks weighing over 20 kg still tied to their

tails, one with a neat bow. They had done their cockpit check thoroughly, but did not check the aircraft as a whole. Another pilot took off with the carburettor heat in hot, when it should have been cold, the mixture control in lean instead of rich, plus the whole aircraft being 60 kg overweight – it never got airborne and two people were killed. Cockpit and pre-flight checks are intended to be memory aids, not a substitute for thought or a licence to forget. There are many pilots who have forgotten to raise their undercarriage after take-off, and then before landing gone through the motions of lowering it, only to find on coming to an abrupt stop that their unthinking hand had in fact finally raised it. It is not, of course, only pilots who need some sort of memory aid, even if it is only a three- or four-letter mnemonic which is easily remembered – more people forget to do their checks than forget the check mnemonic itself. Divers leap into the sea with their air turned off and come spluttering to the surface, glider pilots make record flights only to find they had never switched on the barograph, dinghy sailors put their boats in the water without the bungs in, and canoeists have launched into white water without a paddle. So-called mariners who forget to attach their anchor warp to the boat are two a penny. It even happened with a nuclear submarine. But it can become costly, as when a balloonist forgot to remain in the basket until the next passenger had got in to replace his weight; up it went with a faithful helper still hanging on to a rope. He got a damaged back. Hang glider pilots have taken off without remembering to clip their harness on to the aircraft. Some fell too far.

Carelessness

Carelessness, the next highest on the score-sheet, is a near relative of poor memory; but not quite the same thing. Carelessness is failure to appreciate that some action is important, or to think – if any thought is consciously made – that there is no difficulty. The careless person may remember his check-list but fail to do it thoroughly, or even at all. There was one pilot who shared a small Cub aeroplane with a friend, went out one weekday to fly it from their airstrip. He pulled the Cub out of the hangar and in his own words did a walk-round the aircraft followed by the normal pre-flight inspection. Satisfied, he got in, started up, taxied the few yards to the strip and opened the throttle to take off. About 50 yds down the runway the Cub swung off the tarmac and fell on its face in the grass, breaking the propeller. Amazed, the pilot clambered out to look at his poor aeroplane to discover that there was no rudder – it just was not there at all. His partner had taken it home the previous weekend to do a paint job on it and had forgotten – here we go again – to tell him. So much for a *careful* pre-flight inspection.

Another pilot, of a balloon this time, inflated his balloon in order to take his friends for a ride. He failed to check the wind direction or strength or to notice that it was now blowing 12 knots with considerable gusts. The balloon rose but also drifted fast downwind towards some 34,000-volt power cables. The owner applied full burn to attempt to clear the wires but the basket touched the top wire. Arcing severed the cables holding the basket to the balloon and it fell 60 ft to the ground, killing two out of the three occupants. It was only a simple mistake but carried a savage price. Carelessness of the most minor sort resulted in a man falling into the sea while transferring from his dinghy to a speedboat. The only problem was that the speedboat's 90-hp engine was running, and in falling he knocked it into gear. The

inflatable inshore lifeboat was launched, took the man aboard and then pursued the speedboat as it raced around the harbour in wild circles, trailing its water-ski ropes. The problem was further complicated when on both the occasions that the lifeboat crew tried to return the man to his own boat he fell into the sea again. Twice the I.L.B. had to ram the speedboat to divert it from attacking the pier. Finally with a long boathook borrowed from a fishing boat the gear lever was knocked out of position.

Problem? What Problem?

Unawareness, or no understanding of the problem, lies between carelessness and ignorance. It is an inability to realise the implication of what might happen, or even what is actually happening.

Unawareness may be inherent in some people – they live somewhat remote from actuality – but more usually it is due to ignorance of the subject. It ranges from parents who appear to be quite unaware that their children are drifting out to sea on airbeds, to the pilot who has got himself into weather conditions beyond his ability to cope with, and who is not equipped to know what to do next. Unawareness of this sort is a complex subject and turns up again in the chapter on learning. At the simpler end of the scale plain lack of imagination is a powerful contributor, as when some men were told to open up and clean out a warehouse for future use. The shed was empty, except for an old door lying in the middle of the floor, which the foreman detailed the men to throw out. They picked it up, one at each end and walked off, except that the second man went straight down a 40-ft shaft, which had been protected by the door.

It is easy to ask why anyone should have been suspicious of what might be under the door; nevertheless it is just this sort of awareness, imagination or even curiosity that helps people keep themselves alive.

Not much understanding of the problem was displayed by two youths who took their girlfriends to their boat without warning, so for a start girls were wearing unsuitable clothes. The boys pushed the small motor boat into the calm water with the girls in it, and left them to park the trailer. Quite gently the boat drifted away. The boys shouted for the girls to start the outboard, which was cocked up with the prop out of the water. But the girls did not know how to do it. The boys then shouted for them to throw out the anchor, which they did. But no one had ever attached the warp to the boat. Finally the lifeboat had to be called out to retrieve them. No harm was done, but this sort of unawareness is commonplace.

It is sensible general practice now for scuba divers to tow a lightweight float to indicate their whereabouts. One diver, finding that in spite of finning hard he was no longer going forward, surfaced up his line to discover a small boat containing a pair of happy anglers tied up to 'the buoy'.

More expensive was the incident in which the pilot of a light aeroplane was startled by a continuous banging after take-off. Thinking the aeroplane was about to come apart, even though

there was no vibration, he decided to hurriedly force-land in a small field instead of returning to the airfield, even though this was close by. He overshot, went over a bank and through a garden, finally colliding with trees and a lamp-post. Result, one unrepairable aeroplane. Cause? The passenger seat lap-strap had been shut half out of the door and was slapping against the fuselage. Even though strange bangings in aeroplanes can be very frightening, the pilot seemed unable to appreciate that the risks of forced landing were likely to be infinitely greater than the risks attendant on remaining airborne for the 3 or 4 extra minutes needed to return to the airfield.

The thing about forgetfulness and carelessness is that they happen so easily. Forgetfulness may occur because the information never got fully hoisted aboard in the first place – like remembering names from a cocktail party, looking for treasure on an underwater wreck site and forgetting about how much air might be left in the tank, or because the matter was not properly understood – such as leaving a car on a road which becomes covered at high tide. Carelessness may result from not taking a map or chart because you think you know the way, or not bothering to do a pre-flight check because only you fly that aircraft and it was O.K. yesterday.

No Responsibility

Irresponsibility, or no sense of responsibility, occurs mostly with the individual who may never have had to take responsibility, and so is unable to cope if he suddenly finds himself in charge of his own destiny. One student pilot hit power wires on take-off and landed back to inspect for damage; sensible. But he then decided to fly elsewhere for the needed repairs in spite of a friend's advice not to go. Eventually the student pilot agreed to leave the matter until next morning. At 11 p.m. that night a power company rep arrived and noticed an aeroplane with an envelope stuck over a wing-tip hole, burn marks on the propeller and wings, and with the airspeed indicator pitot tube missing. An hour later the sheriff arrived to discover that the pilot had changed his mind and gone. Next morning the wreckage was found.

A helicopter winchman once told me that the thing he liked least about his job was retrieving children who had been unnecessarily drowned. A few days after one such incident he was walking with his wife along the beach when he saw two small children afloat in a toy inflatable. They were close to the shore in calm water, but only a few yards farther out a strong wind over the low cliffs was hitting the water ready to sweep seawards anything such as a plastic dinghy. He felt sufficiently concerned to approach the parents to tell them of the risk. The father told him to get lost. After walking to the end of the beach the winchman and his wife returned to find the children now very close to the windswept water. Again he told the parents of the risk and again was told to mind his own business. Then, in his own words, 'I just saw red and shook that father like my dog would a rat shouting at him to look after his children.' Suddenly white faced, the father went away and did.

Irresponsibility is always at its least attractive when it involves other people, as when a pilot took up his friend for some aerobatics. After several loops, and spirals, the aircraft spun into the ground and the passenger was killed. The aircraft was placarded as non-aerobatic, neither occupant was wearing a parachute, and the pilot was not wearing the glasses required by his licence for the correction of vision. Fortunately, not all cases of such gross irresponsibility end with disaster. Last year the wash of a big motor cruiser entering a Devon estuary caused the capsize of a canoe containing two children. At least one person on board was observed to have seen what had happened, but the motor crusier was accelerated away. The fact that the children wore life-jackets and were competent at righting their canoe did nothing to excuse such an act.

One of the facets of irresponsibility is the assumption, conscious or otherwise, that someone else will clear up the mess. Returning from a sortie the pilot of a helicopter spotted a capsized racing dinghy a mile out to sea. The pilot expected the boat to be quickly righted by its crew in the normal manner, but when nothing happened he went down to have a look – and took off this two-man dinghy the helmsman, his wife, three children aged between five and eight, and the French *au pair* girl!

Most irresponsible acts contain an element of selfishness or pride. A few are directly caused by drink. But in activities like flying or sailing the majority are certainly unintentional or isolated occurrences, with the person concerned afterwards finding his own behaviour inexplicable. He simply did not know what made him act that way and the lesson is taken to heart.

There are, of course, other failings which come under the 'pilot error' umbrella. Procrastination, or the art of not replacing temporary bodges, and pride; often well demonstrated for all to see by the yacht aground on a sandbank, with its owner brushing away at the seaweedy hull pretending that he meant it.

2 ◇ SINS OF COMMISSION

Quite different from forgetfulness and carelessness are errors in judgement and calculation. They are often perpetrated by conscientious and careful people, who are capable of carrying out whatever it is they are doing, but get something wrong. The glider pilot misjudges the height needed to reach the airfield and grinds to earth one field short, or the diver miscalculates his bottom time and runs himself out of air before getting back to the surface. Misjudgement and miscalculation rarely happen regularly, like forgetfulness, which is why there is often delay before the error is noticed – the person simply is not prepared for the idea that he could make such stupid mistakes. Misjudgement and miscalculation are, of course, an integral part of the process of learning – you can't learn without making mistakes, but after a certain, and often high, standard has been reached the person expects to be able to go on getting it right – but doesn't. Every now and again the experienced car driver misjudges the rate at which he is catching up on the vehicle in front, or the competent sailor, having consulted the tide tables and his watch, miscalculates the time of high water. Of course there have to be reasons; they include familiarity with the exercise, so it may not receive all the attention it should; distraction – chatting to passengers or feeling unwell; misreading data (see transposition errors, p. 78), or being just too clever.

On arriving over an unattended airstrip a crop-spraying pilot saw sheep grazing on the landing area. As the ground crew had obviously not yet arrived to clear them he decided to do this himself by flying low over them. Familiar with the stern discipline of crop spraying there was no problem in doing a low run over some sheep – except he hit them.

In small aeroplanes probably the two most common misjudgements are taking off without using all the available runway; no longer now safe because the wind has changed, and flying in canyons and among mountains without appreciating until too late that the ground is rising faster than the aeroplane, and there is now no room to turn. Miscalculation in small aircraft is mostly about fuel. With 4,000 hrs under his belt one pilot refuelled his helicopter to the brim for a daylight flight of near maximum range. There should have been enough petrol but in sight of his destination the low fuel warning light came on. Since he was so close he considered he would be able to reach the airfield, so overflew an emergency strip close by. Half a mile short of his goal the engine stopped, and he wrecked the helicopter landing on rough ground. On a cross-country flight the engine of a Cessna died, leaving the pilot suddenly in a silent world. During the emergency landing the aircraft was wrecked. Later the pilot admitted that he must have miscalculated on his times and had flown for 4 hrs 20 min instead of 3 hrs 20 min. He also admitted that the fuel gauges in fact read empty when the engine stopped.

Sometimes Too Late

As has been said the real problem with errors of judgement or calculation is that they are rarely recognised until too late – or nearly too late. The crew of an English yacht returning from foreign ports at night searched the shore for the pair of two red lights marking the entrance. But at such a time there is a lot to do, and while the sails were being handed and stowed and the crew were changing gear, in both senses, for an evening ashore, two fixed red lights were spotted where expected, so the boat was homed in on them. It was dark and not much was expected to be seen other than the town lights twinkling in the distance. Suddenly, from the foredeck came a wild shout of 'Breakers Ahead!' Thoroughly shaken the crew swung the boat around and went to work on the problem; to discover that they had initially misjudged their approach line and then taken the red neon of a fish and chip shop to make up the pair of red lights they had wanted to see.

The First Mistake

Although accidents do happen as the result of single, simple mistakes – skidding off an icy road because you were driving too fast – most calamities result from a build-up of errors, each of them probably quite small, even relatively unimportant on their own. This is usually because the first simple error or failure is either not recognised, or is not admitted. If it has been spotted – finding the new chart bought for the voyage has been left at home, or is accepted – knowing the altimeter is sticky and needs to be constantly tapped, then these things can be compensated for; the voyage plan is modified so as to buy a chart at another harbour before running off the edge of the home sheet, and the altimeter receives attention when necessary. The margins of safe and sensible operation are the same as they were originally intended to be and are intact, without erosion. It is not important that a mistake has been made. It is the non-recognition or non-admission of the initial error, by supposedly sensible adults, which is the first step on the slippery slide towards disaster.

Piling up the Errors

It was in Australia that a pilot went to collect a friend and some equipment with his Cessna. On arrival he found the man delayed in town so it was not until 15.50 that he filed a flight plan giving ETD of 16.30. He had been given a copy of the forecast, but his flight plan showed no wind calculations. The flight was expected to take only 75 min, arriving at 18.00 hrs, but this gave only 15 min of daylight to spare. When the passenger finally arrived, his equipment turned out to be some pieces of cast steel 200 lb in weight. In order to keep them well forward, and the aircraft c.g. within limits, the pilot placed them under the seats, but did not restrain them in any other way. He had so far made not one error, but *three*. The margin of daylight was inadequate, the steel pieces were free to slide forward and jam the controls, and they could affect the compass. So far our friend appeared not to have recognised or admitted any of them. Loading of the equipment inevitably took longer than expected, but as the pilot had broken his watch, he did not appreciate he was now about to take off later than intended. Only about 20 min after take-off did the pilot realise that the sun was rapidly bowing itself out. Checking his friend's watch he found it was now 17.30, and there was nearly another hour's flying still to do. He realised they had no hope of reaching the destination before dark, and considered returning to

Port Hedland, his starting place. But remembering an embarrassing few moments he had had there earlier in the day, in having landed without clearance, he decided to go on to an alternative airfield that he reckoned he could reach before dark. It was only one mile off the aircraft's track line. A little later, as the sun disappeared the pilot saw what he believed to be the hills to the south of his alternative airfield, and descended from his 6,000 ft, hoping to spot the lights of the town. He then saw that although the hills were correctly to the left of his track, the compass was indicating 150°, which it should not have been. He guessed that the aircraft heading was now 240° and so turned on to what he believed was a southerly heading, but the compass needle remained immovable. Realising that he now did not know where he was, he continued to search for the lights of the town, but when the hills which he was using as his reference, vanished into the gloom the pilot decided he must land. His margins of anything resembling safety had now been eroded to such an extent, that there was only one course left open – a near night landing in rough country, over which he would be likely to have little control of his fortunes. Searching around in the dusk the pilot spotted what seemed to be a large more or less flat area about 2 miles across, so he made a low run across it and reckoned it was not unreasonable, being mostly spinifex and small bushes.

Choosing what seemed to be a suitable run the pilot made a precautionary approach with full flap, power on, at about 40 knots. As he touched down it became apparent that some of the bushes were boulders and almost at once the Cessna hit one, knocking off a wheel. After some 100 ft of bumpy ride the aeroplane turned over on its back, the pieces of steel failing miraculously to clobber either of the occupants, who were delighted to find themselves almost unhurt. Meanwhile the non-arrival of the Cessna caused the usual consternation and at dawn search aircraft went out looking. It was entirely fortuitous that one of them saw a flash of reflected sunlight nearly 50 miles to the north of the place that had been chosen as the alternative airfield, and which the pilot had thought to be just ahead. It was also fortunate that it was in the wet season, so there was drinkable water, because the aircraft carried no survival equipment of any kind.

This little exercise included forgetfulness – that steel could affect his compass; carelessness – in carrying the steel loose; misjudgement – in starting the flight so late (the first error); miscalculation – timing and navigation; pride – in not taking the more sensible alternative of returning to his starting point. Like a house of cards the errors mounted up until there was no alternative to disaster. But the cardinal error, from which everything accumulated was in taking off for a destination which allowed too little margin of daylight – only 15 min. He should have decided either not to start until the next day, or to have planned to go only to an intermediate airfield. This he could have reached with enough margin to have coped with such things as slightly delayed take-off, or navigational diversions due to getting just a little lost. He did not, so when his inflight problems accumulated he had to try to sort them out in a real hurry before it was totally dark, and in any case had to make an emergency landing with insufficient light to see what the ground was made of.

In case it is felt that flying is a complex matter and that people who do not want to get themselves into such difficulties do not fly, it should be appreciated that the slippery slope which follows any uncorrected initial mistake applies regardless of what is being done. An experienced man in a sailing dinghy gave the tiller to a beginner crew who had never steered a boat before in a fresh wind and choppy sea. This was the first mistake – to hand over control in conditions and on a point of sailing, running with the wind, with which a beginner could not be expected to cope. It was a careless mistake, although easy to understand, and it could have been quickly retrieved by a guiding hand on the tiller or taking the tiller again himself. Neither was done, with the result that the boat shortly afterwards capsized. Neither was wearing a life-jacket, although two were on board lashed out of the way (mistakes 2 and 3). The bailer was not tied in (mistake 4) and drifted away. The two righted the dinghy and the owner then left it to swim several yards *upwind* to get the bailer (mistake 5) while the windage on the boat drifted it out of reach. The beginner in the swamped dinghy did not know that the only possible way of keeping the boat near the helmsman was to capsize it again. Why should he? Instead he got out a life-jacket, put it on and thought of swimming what was now several hundred yards to his friend with the second life-jacket. It was as well that a passing boat picked up the now exhausted helmsman, as the beginner had put on his life-jacket the wrong way up.

3 ◇ HOW TO MANAGE YOUR LIFE

If calamities invariably happen so frequently from a succession of mistakes or failings – some well supported by Murphy's Law – then there has to be a name for it, and there is: mismanagement. In almost every accident mismanagement of the situation was right on hand, sometimes commencing hours, days, or even weeks earlier – like buying equipment that would not be suitable. As one aeroplane instructor remarked of a certain pilot, 'His initial mistake was ever to take up flying.'

The only way to avoid creeping mismanagement is to look on any operation in its entirety; as something which has to be prepared for, thought about, and *managed*. It may be difficult to consider a short dive to look for a weightbelt that was accidentally dropped as a management problem, but that is what it is, no more, no less. There are, of course, many people who automatically prepare for and carry out whatever they do in a methodical manner. They are natural good managers, but most people find that shortage of time, interruption, forced changes of plan, bad weather, not enough cash, and all the other confusions of ordinary life too often put paid to attempts to get as organised as they would wish. Yet others are not naturally managers at all. Take, for example, a routine shopping trip. It is a straightforward management problem, often carried out unconsciously, but a management problem nevertheless. It involves:

1 Deciding the best time to go shopping (urgency of need, parking, other commitments).
2 Preparing a shopping list, and mentally putting the shops in logical visiting order.
3 Putting on suitable clothes, and taking cheque books, money, bags as necessary.
4 Buying what is needed, and deciding alternatives to what is unobtainable.
5 Returning home, checking purchases, and putting everything away.

Translated into a sail or a flight involves the same process:
1 Deciding the best time to go (weather, health, other commitments).
2 Preparing a plan, and putting various intentions or exercises in order.
3 Putting on suitable clothes, and taking maps, charts, check-lists.
4 Carrying out the intention as far as is practicable, and/or taking alternative 'in-flight' decisions.
5 Returning, checking over the aircraft or boat and securing it.

Apart from the fact that good management ensures as far as possible that nothing will be forgotten, its main benefit is that it enables operational decisions to be taken in a logical order, and by a mind uncluttered by muddle or doubts. If the first mistake is to be countered, even if it has not been avoided, it is fundamental that correct decisions or appropriate action are taken then and thereafter; so that there is no risk of the slippery slope process starting up all over again.

Management in Practice

The ability to be able to think in difficult circumstances is something that comes naturally only to some people. Most have to work hard at it by broadening their experience, by practice, by obtaining formal training, and by trying to imagine or anticipate problems and solutions in advance; so that when a real problem turns up they have the best chance of coping with it.

One way to study management in this sense is to look at ways in which other people go about things. In central Australia summers are extremely hot and a lost glider pilot could soon die of dehydration if he arrives on the ground far from shade or help. But one pilot, having got lost through carelessness and poor navigation survived because after landing he managed to make no further mistakes. He stayed quietly, lying under the shadow of the wing with minimum movement, urinated on his clothes to obtain any evaporation cooling that was possible, and mentally composed himself to wait with patience. He was found alive two days later. But, also in central Australia, an immigrant family whose car had broken down, died of dehydration with water still in the car radiator. Their preparation for the trip may well have been adequate, but when something went wrong they were simply not good enough at managing their resources. More recently, the pilot of a small aeroplane had his engine stopped because he had failed to prevent the formation of ice in the carburettor air-intake. Although inexperienced, he had been well taught to fly, even though he had forgotten to use carburettor heat, and he made a forced landing on a desolate and exposed snow-covered upland without damaging either himself or the aircraft. Very creditable: he had made a mistake and then countered his error as well as he could. He now tried to put out an emergency call on the radio but on receiving no reply realised that he would probably have to spend a very cold night in the aeroplane. So he thought he would see if the engine would restart, and if so he would taxi to a more sheltered position. It did start, because the intake ice had been melted by the residual warmth of the engine; but this was the last sensible thing he did that day. His flying training had not covered this sort of situation, and neither had his imagination. He was on his own and not well versed in dealing with unexpected near-survival situations. He climbed back into the cockpit to taxi but the wheels quickly clogged with snow. So he got out to clear them, without stopping the engine although there was now no reason why it should not re-start. This created a new No. 1 mistake. The two main wheels were quickly cleared and the pilot moved to the nose wheel, close to the idling propeller which he had forgotten about. It hit him on the head, cutting his scalp severely. Automatically he put up his hand to defend himself and lacerated three fingers. This blow threw him over and the propeller cut into one foot. Now he was not only marooned but badly injured. He struggled back to the cabin entrance to try to get the first-aid kit but could not climb in – and the first-aid kit was fixed on the back of the cabin wall. The only possibility now left was to somehow get down into the valley and hope to find help. After two agonising miles he found a house and there was someone at home.

Visualising the Scene

These last incidents had one thing in common – a sudden and large change in the circumstances in which people found themselves – and there is no doubt that such traumatic changes can severely affect the ability to think logically, or to continue to think at all. But however straightforward the action seems every effort should be made to avoid later mismanagement by thoroughly thinking over possibilities in advance.

A few years ago a middle-aged couple decided to take their small motor cruiser out of the sheltered Dart estuary, around the exposed rocky headlands of south Devon to the harbour of Brixham, 8 miles away. Although calm in the harbour, off the headlands the wind became fresh and the sea rough – a not unusual situation around headlands. After a while the wife decided that she did not want to continue the trip, and suggested that she be landed on the beach and, local girl that she was, make her way up the cliffs and walk into Brixham. The husband beached the boat and escorted his wife up the cliff, or rather some of the way because she became exhausted and could not go on up – or back down. He left her in a secure position and, now late in the afternoon, made his way to the top and walked in the growing dusk to a cottage for help. The coastguard was telephoned, after which, with a borrowed torch the husband endeavoured to return to his wife in the dark. Inevitably he got lost on the cliffs, and then became stuck so that now he too could go neither up nor down. Eventually, the coastguard found them both and brought them to the top. History does not relate what happened to the boat. Mismanagement included:

1 No proper preparation, inadequate weather information, no alternative plan.

2 Embarking on an unthought-out change of plan involving an impractical solution.
3 Further change of plan forced by failure of previous change of plan.
4 Unnecessary contributory risk by deciding to look for wife in the dark.

Mismanagement Plus

Another occasion which was mismanaged with remarkable consistency was Michel's crash in France, although he had embarked upon this flight with careful preparation. Unfortunately, some of his pre-flight decisions, which were made as precautions, were erroneous.

Before starting Michel went twice to the control tower to study the weather for his trip to the coast with his wife, daughter, and her girlfriend. Although he had qualified for his instrument rating a few months previously he was inexperienced at cloud flying. The Met man told him of frontal cloud on his track, so as the auto-pilot was unserviceable and there was risk of icing in cloud, Michel decided that it would be prudent to fly only underneath – although the forecast was not likely to remain suitable for this. His first mistake had now been made, although it was not serious on its own. At 16.00 hrs he took off, but before arriving at Lyon, where he hoped to join the Rhône valley, Michel found himself faced by a wall of cloud. Unable to go through it he decided to fly along the valley to the west, and passed St Etienne still looking for a chance to reach the Rhône. South-east of Puy, now in really low cloud, he noticed a hole just large enough to climb through and went up into the sunshine on top at 9,500 ft, but without knowing his exact position.

He now committed his second error. Finding himself at a flight level at which he should have been on an instrument flight-plan he reckoned that the most important thing to do was to immediately warn Air Traffic Control of his presence in order to avoid any air-miss incident, instead of concentrating on taking his bearings. He therefore contacted Marseilles who referred him to Montpellier, and after that he was too involved with the radio to locate himself. Now connected to the reassuring atmosphere of contact with control he was taken aback when Montpellier asked him for his estimated time of arrival. Recovering himself, not wanting to look amateurish – and a little frightened – Michel rapidly calculated the time from his original flight-plan and gave this without any further checking. Immediately Montpellier gave him authorisation to descend. Belatedly he tried to check his position by radio beacon but without success. Although Montpellier had no radar he was reassured by the relaxed voice of the controller, and concentrated on descending through cloud without worry – and ignorant of the fact that the headwind was now up to 40 knots (75 km/h) and that he was not nearly as far south as he imagined.

It was his wife, staring into the swirling cloud, who first shouted about houses immediately below. Michel reacted fast by increasing power and climbing, again entering cloud. He was now so scared that he set the engines for optimum speed instead of for maximum speed; and his right hand was still on the throttles when they crashed.

When Michel opened his eyes he was still mentally in command, until he saw the bent propellers. His head was humming so loudly he thought they were still flying, so the bent propellers were a mystery to him. The aircraft had come into contact with the ground at 1,500 m altitude, where the slope of the rising ground corresponded almost exactly with the angle of climb. They had decelerated from 120 knots (222 km/h) to stop in 40 m. Had it been 2 m higher the aeroplane would have missed the top of the mountain, but 2 m lower and they would have been dead. Michel had cuts caused by the windscreen shattering, his wife was cut above the left eye and had damaged several vertebrae, while both the girls had sprained ankles. None of the injuries was serious but the flow of blood was impressive.

Recovering himself Michel first switched off the ignition. Outside, the ground was covered with snow which blended with the cloud making it impossible to see what was what. The aircraft was badly damaged but apart from the door, opened by the shock, the cabin remained complete. With the aid of clothes from their baggage they tried to plug all the holes as night was falling and it was very cold. They did not try to leave in the dark.

Connecting up the radio again Michel put out a mayday distress signal, which was picked by an overhead jet which promised to relay it. Montpellier was in a panic and asked if the survivors could not walk down to a village, as to search for the aircraft that night was impossible. The only useful information that could have guided rescuers was not mentioned by the pilot: the snow. It was the only area in the region where there was any.

Without this valuable information the dawn search was made 100 km to the east, where the jet pilot had noted the best reception of the mayday call, although that does not mean so much in mountains.

The family made an inventory of everything on board. There were just two sweets left so they cut one in four. As soon as it was light in the morning Michel attempted to go for help but visibility was still bad and his legs felt so battered that he fell with each step. After 15 min he returned exhausted, having just been able to make out a valley. After a rest they organised a second attempt. In addition to his summer shirt and flip-flops – scarcely suitable for a wintry wilderness – two glove face flannels were used to protect his hands, leather from the seats made shoes, the cover from a life-jacket, a hood, and the cabin floor lino became a mac. Michel removed the compass and towards midday, with thinner cloud, he set off. He went very slowly trying to remember his route so that rescuers could find the aeroplane. At last the slippery slope of errors had been halted. Where the mountain was steep he rolled to save his ankles, and after a while he could vaguely make out a village in the valley. Now he used a river-bed to walk along as the snow gave way to mud. Finally he arrived at a hard road and 50 m farther on saw people. Ten minutes later he was drinking hot soup at a farm, and two men had gone to find the aircraft.

Perhaps the main point about all these calamitous episodes is that they started out as ordinary weekend fun activities. They were not expeditions to the ends of the earth, nor in any way inherently hazardous enterprises. They became so because the people concerned had failed to realise how very easy it is to make mistakes, and that as soon as the first error has been perpetrated margins which normally exist start being eroded, increasing the probability of future errors as one thing leads to another. They were all examples of simple mismanagement by people who had failed to realise that the opposite of mismanagement is management.

4 ◇ FURTHER CONFUSIONS

As well as the simple human failings like carelessness, forgetfulness, ignorance, pride, stupidity and thoughtlessness, which are an integral part of daily life, others not usually on the surface emerge almost as soon as we get airborne, or descend beneath the waves; and yet others turn up as soon as more people are involved. These failings include apprehension, fear, get-home-itis, the desire to live dangerously, overload, peer pressure and the more specialised versions of the herd instinct. All, except apprehension, are a good potential source of accidents.

Apprehension and Fear

Apprehension is normal and may develop prior to any happening which contains elements of the unknown, or which may be risky, or uncomfortable – like going to the dentist. The effect of simple apprehension varies with individuals – some feel scared, some get a strong feeling of wishing to be somewhere else, and others of becoming an onlooker. Normally, apprehension fades when whatever it is that has caused the apprehension actually starts. It is replaced with a feeling of no turning back, or a 'let's get on with it', and then usually evaporates altogether. It also generally disappears as the person gains familiarity and experience in what he is doing. Apprehension turns up frequently in learning and is looked at again in Chapter 6 (Learning). *Fear* is different, and conscious effort may be needed to control it; otherwise fear turns to panic, which is about the quickest road to disaster. As a submarine escape instructor said, 'There is nothing empties a man's mind faster than being under stress and under water.' Fear, like apprehension, is engendered by the unknown, but it mostly results from not knowing, or not being able to think what action to take. Being 'paralysed by fear' is not really physical, but a massive block in the mind, which suddenly won't produce any answers. A person is unable to force himself to think clearly, he loses control of the situation, and of himself. Fear is best dealt with by sound training – learning how to act in an emergency with confidence, and by exposure to moderate risk situations – preferably at a controlled rate. The essential thing is that both the risk and the fear are recognised, so that they can be assessed and analysed – and dealt with. Like apprehension, the feeling of fear, or being frightened, is a normal human one. If a person is apparently fearless, he probably also possesses little imagination. And without imagination he will be incapable of visualising the scene, of planning what he would do in emergencies, or even of recognising an emergency before it is too late to do anything about it. Although feelings of fear are common to almost everyone, people vary widely in their ability to deal with it. Some cope well in a sudden, short-term emergency, and others do better in long-drawn-out dramas. The sort of people who are good in the quickly come-quickly go emergency are usually those with fast instinctive reactions, although good training helps and for the more sophisticated type of activities, such as scuba diving or flying, is essential. They are people who tend to move quickly physically, are more often young than old, who can keep a clear head uncluttered by imaginative forebodings, and who are competent at what they are doing.

Suddenly the wing broke. Aerobatic pilot Neil Williams had flown one practice aerobatic sortie and took off on a second one with full fuel tanks.

The sequence was flown twice through satisfactorily, and the aircraft was climbed for the next and final run-through. Everything progressed normally until the completion of the fifth figure, which was a vertical climbing half-roll, half outside loop to a vertical dive, and pull-out to level flight at about 1,000 ft (300 m). During this pull-out, as the nose came up to the level attitude, with 5 g indicating, there was a loud bang and a severe jolt was felt through the airframe. I have heard eyewitness reports in which the aircraft is said to have 'staggered'. That is perhaps the best way to describe the immediate sensation following the failure. At the same instant there was a sudden and very peculiar increase in slip-stream noise, and I found myself leaning against the straps to the left although, as I looked left, the aircraft appeared to be flying level.

I had reduced power and centralised controls instinctively at the first signs of trouble.

The reason for the sensation of being pulled to the left was very soon apparent. Although the left wing was flying more or less level, the rest of the aeroplane was rolling left around the failure point. At this stage there was some degree of control over the aircraft, which was by this time beginning to lose height. I throttled fully back to reduce speed and thereby reduce the flight loads, but this caused the nose to drop further. Dihedral was increasing steadily and the roll and yaw to the left were becoming progressively more determined. Full power was then applied in an attempt to get the nose up, but this had no affect at all on the situation. By this time the aircraft was outside the airfield and losing height fast. It was my intention to try to keep the wings as level as possible and to try to achieve a shallow flight path with the intention of arriving, if possible, right way up in the most convenient field available.

It was, however, apparent that if control was being lost at that rate, it would have gone completely before reaching the ground. In fact all control was finally lost at about 300 ft (91 m). At this stage the aircraft had turned left nearly 90° from its original heading, and was banked 90° to the left (at least the fuselage was). I thought the wing had folded to about 45° but it was probably less than that, if one takes into account the fright factor. Full aileron and rudder were being held on and the throttle was wide open as the bank reached 90° left and the nose finally dropped. The sideslip was very high, and the instinctive reaction to pull the stick back only worsened the situation. I had heard a report from Bulgaria some years ago where a top wing bolt had failed on an early make of Zlin whilst under negative g and that the aircraft had involuntarily flick-rolled right way up, whereupon the wing came back into position, and the aircraft was landed by a very frightened, but alive pilot. I had guessed by this time that a lower wing bolt had failed and that I was faced with a similar situation, albeit inverted.

It seemed that if positive g had saved the Bulgarian, negative g might work for me. In any event there was nothing else left to try. I centralised the rudder, rolled left and pushed, still with full throttle. The wing snapped back into position with a loud bang which made me even more concerned for the structure. Immediately the negative g started to rise and the nose started coming up. Altitude was very low by this time and I had no instrument readings at all. For just a moment I thought I was going into the trees, but then the nose was up and the machine was climbing fast, inverted. I was just beginning to think that I might make it after all when the engine died. I checked the fuel pressure – zero. A check around the cockpit revealed the fact that the main fuel cock had been knocked off. This could possibly have been the result of the jolt which accompanied the initial failure. I think I was probably thrown around in the cockpit and may well have accidentally knocked the cock then. I selected reserve fuel and almost immediately realised that this position would take fuel from the bottom of the gravity tank, which was of course now upside down. I therefore re-selected main tank, and after a few coughs the engine started and ran at full power.

I was quite low again by this time and initially satisfied to climb straight ahead. I then turned back towards the airfield and continued the inverted climb to 1,000 ft (305 m). By this time, the remainder of the team had been very quick off the mark and had alerted crash facilities. I throttled back to conserve fuel as I knew the gravity tank was only good for about 8 min safe inverted flight. I then turned the aircraft in steady flight and held the stick between my knees (no aileron trimmer) whilst I used both hands to tighten my shoulder harness even more. Had a parachute been carried I would have climbed as high as possible and used it.

I then considered using undercarriage and/or flaps, but rejected both. Flaps were no use to me whilst inverted, and I could not fly right way up anyway. Also if only one flap extended it would cause an immediate loss of control. The undercarriage required more thought. If I could make an inverted approach with a last-minute roll-out and if the aircraft arrived on its wheels damage might be minimised. However, if the gear fully or partially collapsed the aircraft might turn over. Also, and this was the biggest argument against, the Zlin undercarriage usually extends with a fairly solid thump. I did not know exactly what damage had occurred and I was concerned in case the strain of lowering the wheels might remove the wing altogether. It was just as well that I left the wheels up, because the failure was not the wing bolt after all, but in the centre section inboard of the undercarriage leg.

I also considered four possibilities for landing, namely, inverted ditching, deliberately crashing inverted into the trees to take the impact, inverted crash-landing on the airfield, or an inverted approach with a last-minute roll to right way up and hope for the best.

The last seemed to hold the best chances for survival, so I decided to experiment to see which way was the best to roll-out; if the rate of fold of the wing was sufficiently slow it might have been possible to exercise some control over what was obviously going to be a belly landing (I hoped). A roll-out to the left was attempted and the wing immediately started to fold, with the result that the inverted flight was quickly re-established. The roll-out to the right was not investigated, as the left wing was obviously being weakened by these manoeuvres. Also the supply of adrenalin was getting rather low by this time.

A wide inverted circuit was made for the grass strip parallel to runway 23. As the crosswind was insignificant this afforded the best approach clear of buildings and balloons. The threshold was crossed at 112 mph (180 km/h) at about 200 ft (60 m) with the throttle closed. Petrol and switches were left on in case it was necessary to overshoot; also the canopy was retained, since I did not want my height judgement affected by slip-stream. The possibility of a jammed canopy was considered, but the hood is very light, and I felt that I could break my way out if necessary. A slow inverted flare was made and the aircraft levelled as near to the ground as possible.

As the speed fell to 87 mph (140 km/h) a full aileron roll-out was made to the right, and just a trace of negative g was maintained in order to hold the left wing in place. The aircraft responded well to the controls at this stage, but as it approached level flight the left wing started to fold up again. The nose was already down as a result of the slight negative g, and subsequent examination of the impact marks showed that the left wing tip touched the ground during the roll, although this could not be felt inside the aircraft. As the wing folded the aircraft hit the ground hard in a slight nose-down, left-bank attitude. I released the controls and concentrated on trying to roll into a ball, knees and feet pulled up and in, and head down protected by my arms. I had a blurred impression of the world going past the windscreen sideways and then with a final jolt, everything stopped.

All this happened in less than ten minutes.

Fraught Fortnight

It may be the very characteristics that enable people to cope almost magically with the sudden emergency that sometimes makes for lessened ability to deal with the long-term problem, such as a continuing storm at sea, because for much of the time there is little or nothing to be done, and the continued inaction results in either loss of patience, or a gnawing away at nervous reserves, or both. Such frustrations are good fertilisers for fear. If the need for action later becomes overwhelming, the chances of a wrong decision being made, usually for the wrong reasons, will be increased. The sort of people who in general cope better with longer-term problems are those possessing considerable mental stamina and a refusal to be rattled. They are sometimes, but not always, a bit older. Some quick thinking may be necessary but such people have the ability to make a sensible plan, and after due consideration of the needs are able to change it for a better one at a time when all hell is let loose around them. They are capable of taking a needed rest or meal, because it is sensible while still scared.

Hit by a whale. Round-the-world sailor Bill King's story illustrates this well:

In December 1971 I was attempting to sail my 4½-ton junk-rigged schooner *Galway Blazer II* single-handed, non-stop from Fremantle, West Australia to Plymouth, England, via south of Australia, New Zealand and Cape Horn. At about 16.00 hrs on 15 December 1971, I was about 200 miles SSW of Cape Leeuwin, West Australia, with a southerly wind of force 5 or 6, just free of close-hauled on the starboard tack, on a course to take me south of Tasmania. I was down below doing some chore when there was a horrible scrunch, and a circular portion of the hull, 2 or 3 sq. ft in area, mushroomed inwards like a giant carbuncle with jagged rents through which the ocean started to spurt and pour; one rib was sprung inwards, from a concave to a convex form, but its fibres held.

I wasted a few precious instants by popping my head out of the hatch trying to see what had hit me: without success. I then threw the boat over on the other tack and thus the damage, previously under water, came into the air. I kept full sail on the boat, pressing her hard down on the new, port tack, and had I not been able to do this, the boat would have sunk rapidly. I then pumped out the rising water in the bilge; this took a long time with the handpump, but only an occasional wave was now washing through the holes: the main inrush had stopped.

I had believed in my heart of hearts that damage of this sort could not be survived. I was thus mentally unprepared for correct action and, further, did not have sufficient equipment to deal properly with it. One of the results of this was that I wasted effort in trying to pass a mayday distress call, which, in the event, was never received; and also finally sacrificed a great deal of repair efficiency trying to keep my radio set serviceable.

I got out the storm jib and tried to place it as a collision mat over the hole. After a frightful struggle, I got it over the damage, hauling the head taut under the keel. The sail was too large and clumsy to adapt itself to the wineglass shape of the hull and as the boat was sailing along fast it simply acted as a water scoop, increasing the inflow. To decrease speed would mean putting the hole once more below the waterline; so I reluctantly recovered and stowed the sail. I then decided to stuff some sponge rubber and towels into the holes on the outside and nail a piece of terylene cloth over the damaged portion. To do this I had to hang myself upside-down over the side, with a rope round my ankles and my head in the waves. The nails were long, small-headed, bronze boat-builders' screw-nails. I found it very difficult to hammer them in correctly in this position. I made further attempts by hanging part of my mast-heading rope ladder over the side, and finally, the most successful, the bosun's-chair in which I could sit and lower myself sideways into the water to hammer. I did not make much of a job of it and had to continually break off for pumping.

I then tackled the inside by stuffing some rubber strips into the worse of the rents and, cutting a shore from a spare main boom, wedged it hard against the sprung rib and across to a strength member on the opposite side of the boat. At the same time I was making futile efforts at a mayday transmission. By now it was nightfall and I sat all night pumping, controlling the level in the bilges.

Next day I started to pass 'collision mats' over the damage, making them fast by downhauls under the keel. The first was a waterproof covering cut off the cabin lockers. It was about the right size, but rectangular, and refused to adapt itself properly to the shape of the hull. To 'persuade' it I undergirt the boat with more ropes on top of it, thus clasping it to the ship's side; over this I tried a pair of waterproof trousers: rather too small and only a medium success – this was also well clamped in with more ropes. Finally, I hit the right size and shape; the triangular clew piece of the storm jib. I unpicked this from the sail, used the luff and leech tapes as attachments for the lowering lines and the clew eyelet for the bottom lines; this, when again well undergirt and all hove up taut, really made a good job, and I could reduce sail and also my pumping activities. As well as the lines attached to the mats themselves I now had thirteen ropes running under the keel. I found that I could get them bar-taut by lying on the deck, getting my feet on the toerail and hauling with the strength of my legs, using my arms as links.

In between my efforts at the external repairs I tackled the inside. There were broad strips of thin copper over a good deal of damage. These were essential parts of the radio: two strips which covered the lower parts of the hull were earthing pieces which I cut away. Two others led up into the bows to fire the radio waves up the aerial. These only covered the upper portions of the damage and I could get my fingers in behind them, with some difficulty. I decided, wrongly I think, to leave these in the hope that I might sometime pass a distress message. I also had to demolish some precious lockers in the hull. I stuffed strips of rubber tape into the rents, cracks and holes, and then made up a seaming material out of my disposable pants. Finally, I discovered some sticky yellow tape: I believe it is called mercury chromate, but I have since been unable to find my source of supply or get it replenished. Most forms of sealing compound will not adhere to a surface over which water is pouring, but this – God bless it – did.

I then made up a complex of wedges over the face of the large inward protuberance; these butted one against another and were pressed down with a starfish of shores, but only softly wedged home so that the splintered wood pressed down on the pliant bedding materials but not so hard that it would splinter off.

After about three days I had a repair which necessitated little pumping unless I pressed her hard down on the starboard tack, putting the high damage under water; then it gushed in and had to be pumped a lot.

My strategy then was to make towards Fremantle, about 400 miles to the NNE whenever I could sail with the hole above water, i.e. running free or on the port tack, or with a light wind only and short sail on the starboard tack, and therefore required a wind anywhere from SSW through W to NE. By the wind charts, westerly winds predominate there, but it blew from the east for a week. I hove-to, therefore, drifting slowly towards Africa, keeping a little foresail up to steady her. I felt confident that a westerly wind would eventuate and that my repairs would hold provided no storm arose.

Finally the wind slowly veered towards the west and I slowly sailed towards Fremantle, arriving off Rottnest Island after a fortnight of somewhat fraught endeavour.

After making a landfall at Rottnest I thought my troubles were over. Not so. The wind blew up to gale force as night fell and I decided to heave-to under the lee of the island. I was then in the influence of the north-going current which prevails inshore, and as the wind had backed into the south, I was being set fast to leeward. At about 02.00 hrs I put on sail and started to beat up towards the harbour. An uncomfortable sail as the boat handled sluggishly with the cat's cradle of ropes round her hull and every time I put the port side under water the leak through the high-up hole started to make water. I was kept busy pumping until 15.00 hrs the following day when I thankfully turned into the fishing-boat harbour, where the Fishery Research vessel produced a very welcome brew of tea.

Although Bill King's problem was without question a long-drawn-out one – it must have seemed interminable – he also acted speedily in the only correct way to overcome the immediate problem of sinking. It is not, of course, profitable to try to pigeon-hole characteristics too much because some people unexpectedly surprise both themselves and others in the way in which they rise to the occasion, however hazardous the circumstances.

Coping with the Unexpected

In most so-called leisure activities the risks need not be other than small provided that competence and conscientiousness exist and these qualities are put to good use. But there must always be some possibility of danger whenever an aircraft is airborne, a boat is at sea, a climber is on a mountain or a diver under the surface, and sooner or later some sort of testing, and potentially lethal, situation will arise and therefore must be expected. It is part of the make-up of any operator that he should be able to deal with the unpleasant emergency as well as enjoy the delights of his chosen sport. This may demand considerable self-assessment, not only in how he might cope in hazardous situations, but how he would go about conquering real fear; difficult to find out unless real fear is occasionally experienced.

One fine day the skipper of a small yacht was gently turning this problem over in his mind as he sat with the sun warm on his back, and got a sudden urge to create an emergency just to see what would happen. Without any warning he threw the lifebelt

in the sea and bellowed 'Man overboard'. To his astonishment there was instantaneous chaos. The person on the tiller put the helm hard over, pinning another crew member by the thigh so hard he limped for weeks afterwards, and gybing the mainsail with considerable violence. His wife, in the act of bringing a tray of coffee from the cabin, narrowly missed being beheaded, as the boom crashed across throwing the coffee into the sea. The remaining crewman, sunning on the foredeck, leapt to his feet, tripped over the jib sheet, and only by quick action prevented himself from joining the lifebelt in the water. There was then stunned silence and for a moment total inaction. The skipper found it all most revealing, and sensible skipper that he was immediately arranged a little teach-in so that if someone really did go overboard total disaster would not follow.

The Desire to Live Dangerously

Some people take up risk sports primarily, and sometimes only, because there *is* risk. They are very rarely irresponsible people, but they genuinely need to challenge themselves, to find out what sort of person they are, or to see how far they can go and still win. Their satisfaction and pleasure is taking on the impersonal and elemental forces of the cold, the angry sea, mountains or the remote air. They see flying or ocean sailing as a personal contest. Since time began there have been such people and they have obtained fulfilment by voyages of exploration, by challenging new high mountains, by test flying, or by deep diving. But, equally, over the years the opportunities for really satisfying natural challenge have steadily dwindled. The world is charted, almost all the mountains have been climbed not once but many times – there may be 100 people on the Matterhorn on a summer day. Test flying, and for that matter almost all aeroplane flying, is now more of a technical exercise, dependent in varying degree on ground control; and deep diving exploration has advanced beyond the range of the amateur. But the urge is still there. A fortunate or determined few get going on the oceans of the world where for weeks on end they can achieve the solitary challenge that they need, but for most people the challenge is difficult to find. About the only way open is to push whatever is going to the limits, which is one of the reasons for the growing increase in white water and surf canoeing, hot-air ballooning, relative work parachuting, competition gliding, wind-surfing, hang gliding, skateboarding and hot-dog skiing – and in accidents. Hang gliding grew explosively as a result of the tight control and high cost in conventional flying, hot-dog skiing from the overcrowding and over-organisation of resorts. The problem with this reason for doing things, plus the frustrations of the ever-lessening opportunities for satisfaction of the basic human need for challenge, is that they may sometimes be carried out in a more dangerous manner than is necessary. The need for challenge is probably strongest when people are young, which is also when they have least experience, and usually a magnificently undeveloped sense of mortality. There is only one way to deal with this very real problem of our time, and that is to increase the opportunities for real challenge, and not restrict and confine them by regulation or public disapproval; even the wildest adventurer usually wants to become skilled and to do things better – so that he can pursue his challenge. The chances of his achieving this must not be taken away.

Get-home-itis and Overload

The second-order confusions humans are subject to, and which sprinkle accident statistics with their special presence include get-home-itis and overload. Get-home-itis is the feeling many people develop as an unreasoning or overpowering desire to return to something familiar. It takes two forms: the result of fear in an emergency situation, as when the inexperienced glider pilot has a launching cable break and tries to return to the familiar take-off point that he has just left, even though rational thought would tell him that he does not have enough height to do so. The scuba diver is likely to head for the surface polaris-fashion in an instant of panic if he chokes on his breath, regardless of the damage that this could do to his lungs. The other form of get-home-itis involves the aeroplane pilot or sailor who wants to get home, or to a business meeting, and who convinces or deceives himself into thinking it is all right to go, the weather won't be as bad as the forecast, that he has enough fuel, that he will arrive before dark, etc. This form of get-home-itis may not start with an emergency, but usually ends with one. There was an old adage which said 'If you've time to spare, go by air.' For the pilot of the small aeroplane, regardless of experience or navigational aids, it is still true. The unfortunate Graham Hill was just such a victim.

The flying and diving instructor well knows the problem of get-home-itis. The new glider pilot is taught always to turn in to land early, while he still has enough height to make the turn, or to land in a good field rather than attempt to reach the airfield through the hedge, and the new diver is trained to breathe out and *never* to hold his breath while ascending. Get-home-itis in the experienced pilot is more dangerous. Training lessons are dim memories, business commitments are part of his livelihood, not his recreation, and he may also have demanding passengers with him. It is a very clear-headed and honest person who will admit to them, and to himself, that the flight will be too difficult, or that the weather is more than he can cope with. So he goes, and the accident books are plentifully laced with tales of woe.

How late can you leave it?

There would have been no problem in the contractor getting home that evening except that a test flight had to be made to check the hydraulic system of his aircraft for a possible leak. None was found and the 500-hr pilot landed the mechanic who had been doing the check and at 16.00 hrs prepared for the flight home. During the delay weather had unexpectedly deteriorated, and then there was a further delay due to a telephone fault in getting through to the forecaster. After a short talk with him the pilot went to the local flight instructor and asked him to look towards the range of hills and to say whether it was practicable for him to sneak low through the gorge. The instructor asked what weather information he had been given and the pilot told him 800–1,200 ft overcast. The instructor suggested he forget about the gorge and either go over the top, filing an I.F.R. flight-plan on the airway if he was equipped to do this sort of flying, or stay on the ground. Not hearing the answer he had hoped for, the pilot did not mention the rest of the forecast: of icing in the cloud and considerable turbulence. The instructor suggested he get the pilot a motel room for the night as it would soon be dark. The pilot then telephoned his home, inquired about the weather there, and was heard to ask whether it would be too late to go out that evening when he arrived. After this call the airfield manager also suggested getting the pilot a motel room.

By now it was dark, but the clouds appeared to be broken with the moon shining through. The pilot decided that with only partial cloud he would go over the top, and at 19.05 took off. At 19.16 he called that he was flying level at 7,000 ft, and at 19.22 that he was picking up a lot of ice. At 19.23 control told him that he was below the safe *en-route* altitude and should climb to 9,000 ft. At 19.26 the pilot was informed that radar contact with him had been lost, to which he replied that he was at an altitude of 6,500 ft and was having difficulty maintaining height. At 19.27 the pilot reported he was at 6,400 ft and a minute later at 6,300 ft but could see the ground. At 19.30, height 5,500 ft, the pilot was asked if he would like to return and on affirmation was given clearance. Control asked him if he was still having an icing problem, and he replied affirmative, he was in trouble. That was the last that was heard.

Get-home-itis as a driving force should not be underestimated, and it is extraordinary the length to which intelligent sensible people will go to return home, or to what they believe to be security – a sort of nest syndrome.

One evening the occupants of a small motor cruiser were trying to get home in a foggy last light when, in their hurry to arrive, they went aground on a sand-bar in the estuary. There was no danger since there was no wind at all, and in a couple of hours the returning tide would float them. All they had to do was to anchor and stay put in the little cabin until daylight came and the fog thinned. They anchored, but in the silent solitude of the foggy night the eeriness of their situation was too much for them. The desire to reach something familiar overrode anything resembling logical thought, or even the actual security of their sand-bar. So, they all set off in the dinghy in the fog and in the dark to try to go home. Off they rowed in the direction they knew would take them to the nearest real shore, but without a compass or any visual reference and in a tideway, it was not surprising that the shore did not appear as expected. Around dawn a fishing boat found them drifting, cold and hungry.

Sometimes, of course, the most sensible action that can be taken on any sort of voyage or expedition *is* to turn back, to return home. But it is sensible only when the decision has been arrived at after a logical and reasoned assessment of the situation. There may be many reasons, illness or injury to a crew or passenger, continued adverse weather or simply a belated appreciation that the operation was ill advised in the first place.

Overload

People get into overload situations in their homes. Too much is happening at once, too many things are demanded of them at the same time. It is not possible to cope with it all. Relief takes the form of burst of anger, a strong drink, or throwing the flower vase at the cat. In the air there can be no such relief; the overload situation has to be managed or control of the situation is lost. Overload situations of course also occur at sea and elsewhere, but the air is unique in that it is absolutely not possible to stop and think. Since the overload is invariably one in which getting back to terra firma forms a major part and since the aircraft carries only limited – sometimes very limited fuel – there is no let-up. The overload problem is dangerous because many pilots believe that they will be able to cope – they are instrument rated, are happy flying at night, have flown in bad weather before, have no navigational problems. They know about the effects of icing, hypoxia, and can calculate their fuel consumption, etc. It is only when all their, probably considerable, skills are demanded at the same time that a slip-up occurs – usually it is something quite small, like switching over to the tank the contents of which they have just been thinking about, instead of the one intended from earlier calculations. Or when two people in a light aeroplane were caught out by gloom and approaching darkness, because as their difficulties mounted they forgot to take off their dark glasses. They even missed the runway lights that they were looking for.

No Navigation, No Fuel

Some years ago a pilot was trying to fly an open-cockpit, non-radio aeroplane from northern France to Thruxton airfield in England to have it prepared for a race. The weather was not good but the Channel crossing was made without problem, and a landing made on the English coast at Lympne aerodrome. Weather information was obtained, with the pilot advised to land at Shoreham, some miles along the coast, to check on the extent of the expected deterioration. The weather at Thruxton was still acceptable although cloud base was low. The pilot took off, and squeezing between showers reached Shoreham in a sky that looked harmless except for a dark mass of cloud ahead to the west. Since there was plenty of fuel and Thruxton was only a one-hour flight away the pilot decided to continue on without landing for the weather check.

Within a few minutes, however, as the Downs were reached, cloud base dropped considerably in a sky of menacing appearance. With confidence but not too much experience the pilot continued generally on course, flying around the heavier showers. An unknown reservoir was passed, but the pilot did not feel that there was a navigational problem – yet. The cloud continued to lower; forcing the pilot to lose height to keep at least some of the time in the clear. Thoughts of possible higher ground ahead began to nag. It now started to rain heavily and the air became wildly turbulent. At this moment the map fell to the floor and disappeared under the seat. The expected known high ground was now just ahead and the only way to avoid it, and any obstructions sticking up from it, was to stay in the cloud and above 2,000 ft. Trying to concentrate on flying by instruments, of which the pilot had not done very much, was confused by obtruding thoughts – such as the altimeter would now be over-reading due to lowering air pressure, showing height the pilot had not got. Suddenly the compass needle was discovered to be spinning wildly. Instead of flying straight over the hills the aircraft was turning aimlessly, and setting itself up for the classic in-cloud loss-of-control situation, inevitably to end in a spin or spiral dive. Near panic, the pilot managed to try to think what to do and managed to get the compass to calm down and show a more reasonable heading. Now the engine began to cough and at the same time the pilot realised that the speed had got out of hand in a dive. The clouds swished apart and just ahead was a tree. Shaking with fright as well as being tired, cold, and wet, the pilot pulled up violently, but not enough to vanish again into cloud, although there were wisps all around. Now over lower ground again the weather did not seem quite as awful. Suddenly the pilot caught a glimpse through the murk of a hangar with an army truck beside it – and thought it was recognisable as an airfield not far from home; but decided not to land, as other pilots had previously been ragged for landing there by mistake!

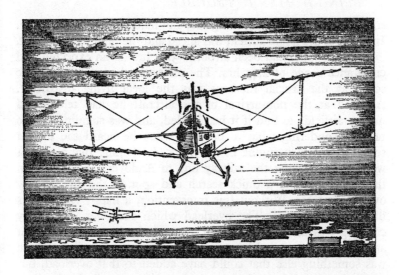

Decision was made to continue the flight as it now seemed possible to stay low over the flatter country; but to where? The pilot was now completely lost and flying at random, although on a hopeful compass heading. Landing in a field was considered, but an unobstructed one could not be found, so the pilot decided to fly more slowly to conserve fuel, which in a muddled way brought the realisation that no fuel check had been made for a long time. There was less remaining than expected – as account of time had also been lost – but the situation was not yet critical. A town appeared below, which the pilot tried hard to believe was Andover, until an avenue of houses appeared that the pilot recognised. It was Salisbury, 18 miles away, and with its 400-ft cathedral spire in the murk. But there was a railway line from Salisbury to Andover, so latching on to this aid the pilot set off for Andover, and from there turned on a compass heading for Thruxton. Nearly home! The pilot leaned back, breathing a sigh of relief, and checked the fuel. Zero. But for how *long* had this situation existed? Worrying now about fuel, concentration on navigation was again lost, and so once again was the pilot. It was essential now to find a landing field before the engine died; just to get back on the ground somehow. With rational thought fast disappearing the pilot was in a daze when another aeroplane suddenly appeared flying alongside, and made a 'follow-me' wave. In minutes the home airfield was ahead and the pilot landing on it.

The aeroplane had been airborne 3.05 hrs on an expected fuel endurance range of 2.45 hrs. The pilot who had arrived on the scene at the crucial moment was the local flying instructor. Alarmed at the non-arrival of the aircraft he had telephoned nearby airfields to find if it had landed, and was standing on the tarmac wondering what to do next when he heard the distant sound of a Gipsy engine in the murk. Reckoning that the pilot would be following the railway line to Andover, he took off in that direction, did a quick search and spotted the aircraft low over some trees. Without this intervention, a happy end to this flight was doubtful. The overload which the pilot was finally carrying was more than enough to preclude the careful thought and judgement needed to carry out a safe forced landing. There was something else that could have added to that overload, but which the pilot did not, fortunately, know about until after landing. In the turbulence a box of non-safety matches had set fire to themselves and burnt up some charts, but owing to the bag being zipped up the fire died.

Overload situations are not confined to the air. The most common in small boats is when a family or group of friends go to sea for a short coastal sail in good weather. The wind and sea become rougher than expected, the crew become seasick and no longer effective as crew, and the skipper is unexpectedly left to cope with sail handling, steering, navigation, tidal study, cold and hunger all by himself. If it now becomes impossible to go into the harbour originally intended, the skipper becomes increasingly less able to do everything right all of the time. It may be a silly small mistake, or occurrence, that eventually leads to the serious end of the problem – like the echo sounder battery dying, and he cannot leave the helm to replace it; and so has to guess the depth of water – and gets it wrong.

Obviously the degree of overload which can be supported varies from person to person, and particularly with the experience they possess. Anyone who remembers learning to drive a car probably also remembers being overloaded by simply negotiating a corner, changing gear, and not running into the car in front all at the same time, yet even a few weeks later, with more experience, there was not only no problem but a conversation could be carried on as well. One of the effects of overload situations with inexperienced operators or some children is that confidence may be undermined if they feel that they cannot cope. Self-appointed teachers should appreciate that their well-meaning activity may be counter-productive if they demand too many actions, or responses, at the same time.

Peer Pressure

Peer pressure is quite simply the effect of the natural desire to do as well as, or better than, the more expert, or to emulate their exploits. It is probably at its most dangerous in sports like hang gliding or skiing where the expertise, or the exploit, is exciting, very visible, and personal. A glider pilot may fly 1,000 km distance, but no spectators see him do it; so although this achievement will stimulate others it does so in an indirect, almost intellectual manner. The exploit of the hang glider pilot or skier much more readily stimulates a feeling of 'if he can do it, so can I'. Most people for various reasons, fortunately do not give away to this super-competitive urge, but a few do; usually people who have not much understanding or experience of the exploit that has so hit their desires. Nevertheless, the temptation by the less skilled to emulate the pundits is real, and needs to be more widely appreciated, especially by instructors.

An indirect effect of peer pressure is that it prevents people asking questions if to do so could make them appear ignorant, particularly in a technical sense. Temptations can best be avoided by a sensible and responsible attitude of mind engendered by good training.

Herd Instinct

In individual sports such as this book is about, it would seem unlikely that lemming-like behaviour would become apparent as a problem; but it does. The inexperienced aeroplane or glider pilot, not all that sure of his position will tend to follow any aircraft that he can convince himself is going to his own destination. Similarly, a sailor will follow another through a harbour entrance, unconsciously assuming that because he is in front he is the more expert. An insidious and little publicised source of accidents, because it may not be mentioned at any inquiry, herd instinct situations are dangerous because the follower ceases, at least to some extent, to remain an independent operator. When the aeroplane ahead suddenly turns away and goes somewhere else the following pilot will have even less idea of his position than he did before; when the following sailor goes aground it is too late to realise that the boat ahead had a lifting keel. Certainly the activities of other aircraft or boats should be studied to obtain information or confirmation, but a commander must remain in command, and at all times act according to the solutions that he works out for himself.

5 ◇ LUCK

This is the moment to say something about luck, that commodity we mostly wish we had more of. Luck plays a quite remarkable part in our affairs and is quite random in its behaviour. Luck, good or bad, is equally *rare*, and what many people put down to bad luck probably has nothing to do with luck at all. Luck is genuine only if the possibility of the occurrence is statistically minute, such as a scatter of mini-meteorites hitting a passenger jet, or could not have been reasonably foreseen and therefore avoided by anyone involved. Some years ago a club member was driving a glider launching winch on his own at the far end of the airfield. Flying was somewhat desultory and as it was a warm day he stood out in the sunshine near the winch while waiting for the next glider to be made ready three-quarters of a mile across an empty field. Suddenly and without any warning he felt a sharp pain in his chest and fell to the ground. When he realised he was not dead he discovered a ·22 bullet lodged against the rib over his heart. It was later found that a farmer 2 miles away on his own land, and with a large wood between him and the airfield had shot up at a rook. The farmer was a responsible person, his rifle was in good condition, and he was licensed to use it on the farm. As far as he was concerned his shot had carried no risk to anyone and he was appalled to find that his descending bullet had hit the only person in the best part of a square mile of empty ground, *and* had struck him over the heart. Such 'luck' could not have been reasonably foreseen or avoided other than by the farmer never firing his weapon upward.

It was also genuine bad luck that killed a man snorkelling in the Mediterranean. He was quietly floating about studying through his mask the colourful fish and Coca-Cola tins on the bottom when a bee settled on the end of his snorkel tube. At that instant the man breathed in: the bee was swept down the tube and into his throat, where it stung him. He suffocated. That was pure random chance.

But it is not chance when a pilot breaks his aeroplane on take-off due to the distracting effect of a painful sting, if he knew there was a bee or wasp somewhere in the cabin before he opened the throttle to go. The pilot should have assumed that the vibration, draught or noise of take-off could easily disturb even a sleepy bee. That accident was caused by the pilot's failure to dispose of a known risk.

Randomness of Luck

It is perhaps in the 'lucky escapes' that the random effect of luck is at its most remarkable. An airman who fell out of a disabled bomber at over 10,000 ft lived because the bit of mother earth he hit at 120 mph was a steep deep-snow slope which decelerated him at just the right rate. More recently a doctor on a mountaineering expedition was cook at the overnight camp at 14,000 ft on Mt Rainier. With everyone else inside the tents he was sitting watching his pots when a gust of wind blew off one of the lids. He went to pick it up, slipped and went over the edge of the steep ice-covered slope – and kept on going for 1,700 ft. Whether or not he was at fault for having slipped is immaterial. He went down a slope varying from 40° to 60° in steepness and covered with rocks. Head over heels he hit them, ricocheted in and out of troughs of ice, tried to grab at anything to stop himself, bounced across several crevasses, and finally went over a sheer 200-ft cliff. At the bottom were huge rocks and equally huge banks of snow: he hit the snow. He was alive, though with a considerable number of broken bones and lacerations, and also almost without any clothes which had been torn off during the fall. He reckoned he would freeze solid before anyone could arrive. His friends found him within two hours, wrapped him in four sleeping bags, and he went on living. In all that totally uncontrolled falling at no time had his head hit a rock.

A canoeist, racing down the rapids of a fast-flowing river with a group of friends, rammed a submerged tree trunk and capsized, trapping himself by the legs with his head a foot under the water. Unable to free himself he knew that he would die – until he discovered that he was still breathing. White water is so called because of its creamy consistency due to the thousands of tiny air bubbles that are generated. As the tumbling water rushed past the back of the canoeist's head it eddied around his face, and in this slower-moving flow the air came out of solution into one big bubble. If the water-flow had been less fast, or the canoeist had been jammed with his head pointing in a different direction, he would have drowned.

Lucky or Accident-Prone?

Some people are lucky, or considered to be so, and others not, but this situation rarely results from random chance. People who seem to be unlucky, are often called accident-prone, because of the way in which they constantly trip over disaster. The real reason is that they are either physically clumsy – some people just do not seem to be aware of where their feet are – or because they are not very good at ordered thought or decision-making – scatterbrained in old-fashioned parlance (discussed more in Chapter 6, Learning).

These people are unfortunate in that in almost everything they do they start on the debit side of the initial mistake. Physically they are more likely to fall overboard, or slip. One diver went down a flight of sixteen wet granite jetty steps on his back with his air bottle crashing on each step: everyone else threw themselves

to the ground, but it did not explode. On the scatterbrain side they are likely to leave something behind, be unaware of the time, or be otherwise erratic. Sometimes it is difficult to know whether an incident or accident was caused by luck or not; such as when a sailing boat in the middle of the ocean is hit by a whale. Certainly the accident would not have happened had the boat stayed at home, but this is irrelevant. There seem to have been an increasing number of such incidents in the last few years, but equally there has also been an increase in small boat ocean sailing. What no one knows for sure is whether the boats are sunk as a result of random collisions with sleeping whales, which would be pure bad luck; whether the whales are curious and do not know their own strength; or angry and deliberately attack. If either of the latter these may be classed as accidents with causes for which remedial measures can be taken.

There is no doubt that the feeling of being lucky or unlucky has an effect on the way in which a person reacts, and therefore affects their subsequent actions and decisions. A person convinced that he is lucky may concentrate less on making the necessary effort, assuming that all will be well; and so he is less likely to be prepared should something unexpected go wrong. On the other hand the person who believes himself to be unlucky is inclined to be less confident, and thus may be indecisive or less competent when things are not going particularly right. He is therefore less likely to take the correct measures. Because of its random nature, there is no reason why anyone should expect to find luck coming their way. 'With a bit of luck we'll make it,' is usually something that doesn't happen.

6 ◇ LEARNING

Thorough learning is needed for anything worth doing; and it is a process which has no end.

Somewhere along the line we have *learnt* what we know how to do, from the simple act of walking to the complex processes of running a committee meeting or flying an aeroplane. Much of our basic learning, such as our first steps in walking, is forgotten; but the more complex activities have been acquired largely by a

mixture of assembling, or reassembling, what knowledge we already have, and building new information on to this foundation. It is inevitable, therefore, that the rate of learning in any new activity, such as diving, and the degree of understanding achieved, will be affected by what knowledge and experience is already possessed. As an example, a person might be expected to learn to dive better or more quickly if he had experience of swimming and other water sports, than if he had never been in any water but his bath. Any background knowledge and understanding of the environment in which he will operate as a diver enables him to concentrate better on both the learning of the new techniques and relating them to existing knowledge and experience. The problem with only theoretical learning of techniques is that although a superficial skill may be acquired, the person will get himself into trouble because he has insufficient understanding and experience of the overall problem.

Craft Skill and Self-reliance

In any activity using complex gear the operator, if he is to obtain the maximum amount of fun and use from his expensive equipment, needs to have very considerable knowledge and understanding in three different areas.

First, he has to learn a craft skill; he has to be able to handle the controls of, say, a glider in a properly co-ordinated manner and fly and land it accurately. This is not a particularly difficult thing to learn given a competent instructor.

Secondly, he has to learn to operate his equipment in an environment – if a glider in the air – of which he probably has little or no previous experience. He not only has to learn how the wind and weather will affect him, but learn to harness their energies in order to soar. He has to learn to operate in three dimensions and deal with new problems of moving, including accelerating and decelerating, in more than one direction at the same time. The learning and understanding of these things is more difficult and takes longer. It demands a considerable degree of self-teaching, because such learning has to continue long after any formal training has finished.

Thirdly, the operator has to develop self-reliance, that mix of technical know-how and animal cunning. He has to be able, however difficult the circumstances in which he finds himself, to think logically, take correct decisions, and carry them out. This demands an awareness of what problems could arise and a constant alertness for signs of potential trouble. It demands sufficient self-discipline to plan and prepare properly, and sufficient strength of mind to avoid being persuaded by others into actions known to be unwise. The development of a strong sense of responsibility, and reliance on one's own resources and decisions may be the most difficult of all to acquire.

Only if and when learning is developed in all these three respects will the operator be able to manage his situation and have a real probability of avoiding the downward spiral of accumulating errors.

He, himself, should be able to recognise any mistakes he may make, cope with the effects of technical failure, and retrieve the situation. Society, with its 'cradle-to-grave' care, and attitude of saving people from themselves, does little to strengthen self-reliance and independence of thought; although most people like to think of themselves as possessing both in good measure. For many, real self-reliance based on sound judgement takes a long time to develop, and as with the understanding of a strange environment, will extend far beyond any likely period of formal schooling. The problem is that during the time, perhaps years, in which this awareness, understanding of the problem, and self-reliance is slowly or steadily growing the operator is at risk. Often he may not appreciate that he is at risk, simply because he has not yet developed the judgement necessary to fully assess and deal with difficult situations. Accidents in air and water are not so much caused by people using their equipment incorrectly in a technical sense, but by getting themselves into situations beyond their experience or ability to control. They fail to assess the situation correctly, or fail to appreciate that conditions are changing, or fail to take remedial decisions either in time or at all.

Skill, but no Judgement

A visitor to South Australia went diving with the locals. The morning sortie had gone without difficulty, although he noted that some things were done differently from the way he had been trained at home, such as diving without A.B.L.J.s (adjustable buoyancy life-jacket), and stowing snorkels in their trunks instead of under the mask strap. By afternoon the weather had deteriorated, the wind was fresh, the swell a metre high, and the sky grey; and someone had drowned earlier in the surf farther along the beach. No one was all that keen to dive, but they finally decided to go, and the visitor went along too, although conditions were now no longer like anything he was used to. He and his buddy partner decided to snorkel out against the current to save air, then dive to 70 ft about half a mile from the beach. They would then turn towards land and enjoy exploring the bottom with the current helping them home. All went according to plan and they made bottom at 80 ft in 25–30 ft visibility. Suddenly the visiting diver had an air stoppage in his regulator which gave him a fright. But it popped clear, and they carried on, swimming easily over the sand and coral. Then he had another stoppage, so he signalled his buddy to go up, and they surfaced together in good order; except that the wind had strengthened, the waves were higher – *and they had been swimming the wrong way* over the bottom. Now, more than a mile from land without a cover boat or any emergency arrangements, they did not have enough air left to return to the beach by swimming in the calmer water under the surface. They agreed to dive to about 20 ft and swim at this depth until their air ran out, when they would continue on the surface using snorkels. A few minutes later at 20 ft the visiting diver's regulator had a further stoppage and this time it did not clear. Back again on the surface, snorkelling was not easy in the rough sea even when the visitor had found his snorkel from the unfamiliar place he had stowed it; and they expended considerable energy choking on the water that splashed into the open-ended tubes. Without A.B.L.J.s to inflate and permit some rest, and carrying both weight-belt and the now-useless tank, the visitor was in trouble. He released his weight-belt and watched it vanish into the depths. This did not help enough, so he abandoned his tank. Even this was not sufficient, as he realised that he had swallowed so much water and used so much energy that he was now too weak to continue to swim on his own. He called to his partner for help, but he obviously did not understand and stayed where he was, about 15 ft away. They were still some 600 m from the shore, no longer drifting towards the beach, but to the foot of high cliffs over which the waves were breaking in pillars of spray. At this moment of hopelessness some beach guards arrived on surfboards, one of their vigilant number having spotted two heads when they crested on a wave.

There was a common chain of errors and failures in this incident, but as far as the visitor was concerned most of them resulted from his failure to assess the situation correctly, and his failure to take correct decisions. He was a competent diver technically, but he first of all put himself at risk by diving without the A.B.L.J. he was used to. He then got led astray by agreeing to dive when the weather and sea conditions were marginal, and more difficult than at home. He failed to retain independent control over his own safety by checking that they were swimming in the correct direction; on such a dive without boat cover, which was in itself stupid, they should *both* have carried a compass. This near calamity was not because the diver had not learnt the technical skills, but that he had not yet developed sufficiently those more elusive attributes of awareness and judgement, of understanding the environmental problems, and even of learning how to say No.

Instant Skill

Accidents in diving, or flying are readily available to anyone, because equipment and leisure time are also readily available. Ease of mobility allows a wide choice, enabling perhaps two or three sports to be 'done' in a weekend. With such variety it is easy to concentrate on the craft skill, either by 'going on a course', or self-teaching, but even easier to fail to appreciate that there is, for example, more to going to sea than simply putting a boat on the water and starting up the outboard. Before the advent of mass-market sports equipment and such widespread opportunity, people who involved themselves in an activity like canoeing or sailing did so because they lived where the water was. As a child they may have had a raft on a pond, graduated to an old self-repaired boat on a river or estuary, and eventually ended up with a respectable vessel. They had no formal lessons, but over the years acquired skill, awareness, and judgement in great depth. Of course the raft had structural failure, the dinghy got stuck on the mud at dusk, and all manner of mistakes were made, but the pond was not very deep, and tides are understood by people who live by them. With no rescue services on tap, and a few long walks home, self-reliance grew. Now most people want to buy the equipment and get going with the minimum of delay, if possible acquiring instant skills on a short course. Some soon appreciate that it is not as easy as they thought, and try something else, others also appreciate this and get down to learning properly, but a few just remain unaware. The effect of 'instant learning' concerned a couple who joined a diving branch and started their basic training. Before this was through they joined some members for a weekend's diving, but were told by the Dive Marshal that under no circumstances would they be permitted to dive together as their experience was insufficient. They complained that they had been diving together all week with another group – having led them to believe that he was qualified and she 'almost'. The Dive Marshal was adamant so, annoyed, they returned to the other group to dive. They went down together to 70 ft, and at this depth the husband ran out of air. His wife shared her air with him, taking two breaths alternately from the same regulator, until they were up to about 30 ft from the surface. Then 'something went wrong' so the wife blew her A.B.L.J. and brought them both to the top, but was then unable to hold him and he sank. When found he was still wearing his weight-belt and empty tank, but his A.B.L.J. emergency air cylinder was missing. It had been lost on a beach three months previously. They possessed the minimum of technical skills, little overall experience, and no judgement.

Regulation or Self-discipline?

Much equipment, as for diving, does not need a large capital outlay, and water lies around all over the place. It is even possible to dive or sail without reading a book. As familiarity grows with the popular acceptance of sport, such a situation if left to itself can only become less safe. But it is not a situation amenable to control by regulation. People do not know all the regulations that already exist, and regulations cannot cover either all eventualities or some eventualities suitably for all people. Excessive regulation not only adds considerably to the cost, but, like penicillin, also breeds resistance.

Unnecessary accidents are best avoided by the ready availability of good teaching by good instructors, whether they be professionals or just helpful friends. There is a self-regulating process with accidents; if the rate becomes higher than seems acceptable some people go and do something else, but others endeavour to find out and learn more. This has happened with hang gliding. To begin with there were a few people who had thought a lot about the problems of such simple personal flying, and because of their deeply dedicated thinking there were also very few accidents. But this sort of flying was so attractive that the growth of the sport became explosive. During the last few years people have been able to build, buy, and fly hang gliders with great ease, but with often no real appreciation of the aerodynamic, environmental or self-disciplinary demands of this – or for that matter any other – sort of flying. People have been killed; almost entirely through failure to understand the basic aviation needs of proper pre-flight preparation, not operating beyond their experience, and not using their aircraft beyond the design limitations. In the beginning the idea of schools, formal training, or proficiency standards was anathema, now it is not only wanted, but expected by newcomers. The current problem is to find enough people who have managed in the time available to gain sufficient knowledge and experience to become good instructors.

7 ◇ TEACHING

The job of the instructor in any sport is basically the same: *to transfer the necessary knowledge and understanding in a manner comprehensible to the student and at a rate that he can handle.* Most bad teaching stems from a failure to appreciate this fundamental principle.

The first essential is that the instructor has the necessary knowledge and is himself competent at what he is attempting to teach. If he is not, or if he cannot answer questions clearly and accurately, the student will soon lose faith in his mentor. This, although undesirable, may not matter too much in quiet water dinghy sailing or canoeing, but is likely to be disastrous in the learning of flying or diving, where the student is in a new element and absolutely dependent for his safety on his instructor. Confidence undermined at this stage may never be fully recovered.

Assuming that the instructor really knows his subject, he then has to communicate the necessary information in a logical sequence; so that the student is able to build first on a foundation of existing experience, and then be able to go on adding new information in a way that relates to what has gone before.

The transfer of the necessary knowledge – communication again – is probably the most difficult part of instructing; often because it does not seem too much of a problem. But it is of no value if the instructor informs with what seems to him to be perfect clarity if the meaning received by the student is different. This happens more frequently than is often suspected, and it occurs because the instructor provides information that the student is not yet able to relate to existing knowledge, or because the phrases or words used by the instructor have a different meaning for the student, or because the instructor has built into his explanation a confusion of emphasis.

Teaching a Two-way Process

It is perhaps memories of the schoolroom, with a teacher droning on and on, that leave the idea in the mind that teaching is simply output from an instructor. Teaching craft-skills, like climbing or flying, must essentially be a two-way process, because if the student does not understand what he is learning his life will be at risk. Teaching must consist of continual lesson-and-response. The instructor provides information or demonstrates some aspect of handling – such as how to hold a canoe paddle, or how to maintain correct airspeed in a glider, and he should not continue with any further teaching until he is sure that this step is properly understood. The student should be questioned to discover how much he comprehends, or to find out what is not clear to him, and he should, of course, be encouraged at all times to ask questions, *however silly they may sound.* By practical skill demonstrations the student should then show the instructor what he has learnt. The demonstration does not need to be very good, provided it indicates that the student clearly understands what he is trying to do. Before the next day's, or week's, lesson the instructor should ask the student to himself provide a brief recap on the learning obtained from the previous session. It is sometimes surprising how the understanding, or even more, the emphasis, of the earlier lesson has been modified by the student thinking about the matter on his own during the interval. Following response from the student, it may be necessary to repeat part or all of the lesson to establish it firmly in his experience. One of the problems of instruction on short (1–2 weeks) courses is that there is a temptation to include too much, so that the course member who has paid a good fee, feels that he is getting somewhere. Over-ambitious programmes leave no time for recapitulation or consolidation, and often result, perhaps also due to bad weather, in sketchy coverage of some fundamental lessons. The student goes home not knowing what he doesn't know.

Teaching at the Right Rate

One of the advantages of the individual teaching of a craft-skill over schoolroom teaching, is that it *is* possible to teach the student at the rate at which he personally is able to learn new things. People vary widely in this respect, and in an unfamiliar environment, like the air, may appear to be extraordinarily slow. This is not because they are stupid, but because so many new impressions and demands are all competing for attention. The instructor has to find out how each of his students will learn best, and initially select for them priorities for their concentration. If the student is also apprehensive, and for many starting a new activity like gliding may have been a big decision to take, the instructor may have to spend considerable time initially in focusing attention on things which will allay this apprehension. Some people are convinced, for example, that canoes, boats, gliders and aeroplanes are all unstable and will turn upside-down without provocation. With such students it is quite useless attempting to teach them to use the aeroplane or boat, until they have themselves convincingly overcome such irrational fears. Other people appear to learn confidently and quickly, and are impatient to get on. Their problem is that learning may be superficial. If this is not recognised, it will probably prove inadequate later when the person is carrying the higher workload of controlling his equipment, dealing with difficult weather, or sea, and having to make vital decisions of policy on his own responsibility. Something goes; the glider is flown at too low an airspeed, or the diver forgets to check his air; or other wrong decisions are taken.

Teaching at a rate at which the student can handle new information and relate it to his existing experience makes considerable demands on the instructor, because the same lesson may need to be presented differently to each student. It is axiomatic in teaching things like flying or diving that only one new exercise is taught at a time, and that this should be properly understood before proceeding further. This may not always be practicable or necessary in simpler activities, but the instructor must always remain conscious of the need to avoid confusion developing in the student's mind.

Too Much Teaching

There are, unfortunately, some instructors who believe that provided they have said everything on the subject, and forgotten nothing, the student has been told, and now knows. This is a real fallacy. It is simply not physically possible for anyone to hoist aboard more than a certain amount of new information at a time, and this may not be much. Of all the pearls an instructor bestows upon a student, most will be lost. The problem for the student overwhelmed by a torrent of strange words and instructions is that he does not know what is important to remember. He wants to learn, but all he finds himself able to do is to latch on to anything which he can relate to his existing experience – and this

item may be quite irrelevant. There is also a tendency by some instructors to hand out lessons on theory, not only too early in a student's training, but in too concentrated doses. It has to be appreciated that for most people theory is easier to accept *after* they have had some practical experience, and are able to visualise what they are supposed to relate to the theory. It also has to be appreciated that learning new things is best consolidated by having *time* in which to consider, juggle, and sort information in the mind. Lessons should therefore always end with indications of priorities for such consideration.

After teaching for some years the most valuable thing any instructor can do to ensure that he is still good at his job, is to go as a pupil on a training course for some completely different sport that he has never tried before. Suddenly he finds himself at the receiving end of a new learning situation, and will gain much from the experience.

Training for Emergencies

In most of the activities with which we are concerned, some training in emergencies is necessary in a simulated form. Dinghy or canoe capsize drill, glider spin recovery, emergency dive procedures or aeroplane forced landings, are examples. It is very easy for this teaching to become a formalised and routine part of the training programme. In doing so it loses much of its value, because it is expected. It becomes an exercise *to do*, whereas in reality the danger lies in its unexpectedness. Certainly it is necessary in flying to *do* spins, so that the recovery drill is learnt, but people kill themselves by spinning *unintentionally*, because their concentration was elsewhere, or because they had become overconfident. When such a spin occurs, it is so unexpected, and the pilot is so surprised, that there is invariably considerable mental delay before recovery action is started. If the aeroplane or glider is low on the approach, the pilot may not even have got around to doing anything, before the ground arrives.

The lesson on spinning needs to concentrate on thoroughly learning what the aircraft feels like when it is flown too slowly for safety; so that the pilot will react instinctively to the symptoms *before* a stall occurs. The capsize evening on the dinghy sailing course, often done in calm water, may be hilarious and is valuable; provided it is appreciated by all that an unexpected capsize in an overpowering wind in a tideway, with a crew who is thoroughly scared, will be absolutely different.

Some instructors get the idea that deliberate harassment in training is useful in making the student aware of the dangers. On balance harassment is more likely to frighten or confuse than teach, particularly if the situation created is artificial – like turning off a diver's air supply or the instructor suddenly putting the aircraft into an unusual attitude. Although a student may be easily scared, he is not usually stupid; he knows that he would not do these things to himself and so is not convinced by such tactics, merely worried. He knows that there are dangers in his chosen sport, and he expects to be taught how to deal with them, but the lesson has to be seen to be necessary. Emphasis on the unexpected aspects of emergencies should come from the instructor's skill as a teacher, and not from dramatic harassment tactics. It is in the area of emergency skills and decisions that the good instructor will get across the need for awareness, the need for the student to learn more about the new medium in which he will be operating, and need for reliance upon himself and his own resources to get, and keep, out of trouble. To start with, the instructor has to do all the thinking for his student, but the student has not become an operator in his own right until he is capable of doing all his thinking – and decision taking – for himself.

Instructor Quality

The good instructor is the most valuable asset in any activity in which poor training can positively add to the hazards. The standing of his sport is largely in his hands, as well as the quality of future instructors. But some people become instructors for the wrong reason. It is a good way of obtaining the flying hours needed to become a commercial pilot, or it provides a feeling of power or status, or it is a way of filling a college vacation. Some excellent instructors have come on the scene this way, but it should not be forgotten that bad instruction is a good killer. No one should take on the job of instructing in any risk activity, unless he is prepared to also carry the responsibility for the lives of his students. Some calamities resulting from bad instruction do not occur during the actual training, but perhaps years later, when some flaw in technical understanding, or wrong attitude of mind, is put to the test. A great deal of teaching is also done by people who are not qualified instructors. People teach friends, parents their children, and club members help other members along. The quality of such instruction, as would be expected, ranges from excellent to abysmal; but the average is often not bad because the personal attention usually devoted makes up for any shortfall in technical expertise. Since such people are sometimes not especially skilled themselves they provide from their own recent experience a good feel for problems and difficulties that arise, and thus an awareness in the mind of their pupil.

Some, of course, teach without realising they are doing so; by example, and what is learnt may be unintended or problematical. A family arrived one night at a south coast rented cottage complete with dinghy on trailer. The public landing ramp was only a few hundred metres from the cottage, so father and son – mentor and pupil – went there to launch the boat, while mum rustled up some supper. The idea was that the son would paddle the dinghy round to the cottage beach where father would meet him, having parked the car. Because it was only a short trip mentor did not think it was necessary to provide anchor, flares, or even life-jackets out of the car – they could do all that tomorrow. Off went the son, and promptly disappeared into the night borne rapidly away by the wind and tide, against which he was quite incapable of paddling. It all ended without too much drama, with maybe both mentor and pupil adding a little something to their experience.

Instructor Mistakes

Instructors can, of course, make mistakes and have accidents just like anyone else. There are two typical areas where they may end up with a red face. One is when an instructor – the acknowledged local expert – is asked to do something for which he either does not have the experience or is out of practice. A gliding instructor, for example, has come to grief giving an aerobatic display at a local airday. Everyone knew he was an expert pilot, good at teaching aerobatics, and knew the district; but the last time he actually did solo aerobatics low down for display was 5–10 years ago and he was reluctant to admit to any lack or loss of skill. The second type of error occurs in the immediate 'pre-flight' phase of a lesson, because at this time the instructor is most likely to be in an overload situation, as were the two instructors running an inflatable dinghy boat-handling course. They had been in the classroom teaching safety drills, basic navigation and engine failure during the morning, and had had a rushed lunch as the inflatable had been in for repair, and all its equipment was scattered about; but finally they reckoned to have got everything ready on time. The class members arrived, launched one boat through the small waves on the beach and paddled out into deeper water to start the 65-hp outboard. It didn't start. 'Right,' said the instructor, 'you have all learnt what to do. First check the fuel system, and if that is O.K., check the ignition. The rest of you keep paddling.' Laboriously two students worked their way from the tank to the

carburettor, while the remainder in wet suits sweated to keep the inflatable off the rocks. 'No problem with the fuel,' reported the students, and moved on to the ignition. And there, where the plugs should have been, were just two round empty holes. Meanwhile, the other half of the class in another inflatable also put to sea – with the fuel tank sitting mutely on the jetty.

8 ◇ COMMUNICATION

'For those viewers with black and white sets, Liverpool are in the red sector' – TV commentator.

Very many years ago I went to an airfield to fly a small aeroplane. In the office, the owner – who was also the manufacturer – was busy. He knew I was coming to fly, and also that I had previously flown one of his products. On seeing me he interrupted his conversation with someone else, and called out to 'take the new one'. I went outside, climbed into the new aircraft, which was easy to differentiate from the old, blue one, that I had flown before. The engine started easily, and off I went for 20 min very pleasant aviation. On my return there appeared to be a certain amount of fluster evident, because the aeroplane I had been flying had not yet been test flown; it was indeed new. The blue one was either what he had said and I had misheard, or what he had meant to say, and had not.

Simple communication failures of this sort happen every day. Occasionally, they result in some disaster the reason for which may be impossible to discover, because there is only one side of the story left for evidence. Usually, which is just as well, there is just confusion, as when after a gale an inshore rescue boat was asked to check on any yachts which had come adrift from their moorings. In doing so the crew took aboard some outboard motors to save them from further damage, and reported to the coastguard over the radio that they had aboard three engines. Within minutes the local press was on to the coastguard inquiring about the three Indians who had been picked up.

English is the official air communication language, with words having precise meanings, but even this is sometimes not enough. One aircraft controller in Africa cautioned an inbound pilot that there was a 'Land-Rover on the right side of the runway'. The pilot replied 'Unnerstan lan ovah on right side of runway'. 'Negative, negative,' cried the controller, 'Land-*Rover* on right side mowing the grass.' Maybe it would have been better to have used the word jeep! Another easy muddle in words occurred when a pilot was waiting to take off at a busy airfield. He understood the controller to say that it was 'All clear' for him to go. He realised that the wording was unorthodox, but there did not seem to be any apparent reason why the instruction did not mean what it said. But what the controller had actually said was 'Hold clear', meaning stay clear of the runway. But 'Hold clear' is not, in fact, good wording, because any loss of the aspirant, particularly for a person whose own language is not English, will give the wrong meaning. It is a hundred years since the Royal Navy became tired of the muddle between the similar sounds of starboard (originally the side of the offset steering oar) and larboard (the landing side of the boat). So they retained starboard, and introduced port: not only a continuation of the original sense of the land, or port, side; but easy to remember, because the colour of drinking port is also red. This breakthrough, alas, has had little follow-up. In flying instruction there is 'I have control' and 'You have control'. There is also Avgas, for petrol, and Avtur for kerosene – recent new inventions. In the French language there is dessus for above and dessous for below and est for east and ouest for west. Not confusing perhaps to the French, but certainly to divers or glider pilots of other nationalities.

Words similar in sound, such as stalagtite and stalagmite, are more difficult to memorise in the correct sense. Words that are dissimilar in sound, even though similar in meaning, are easier to memorise and to get right: for example, huge, big, long, tall; because 'meaning' memory works better than acoustic memory.

Further to the Confusion

Another good source of confusion occurs in the giving of positions or bearings. Glider trailer crews have searched fields to the S.W. of a town for their glider when it was the town which was actually to the S.W. When giving the position of a boat or a person in the hills, it is important that the information provided will always be interpreted in the same sense. So much muddle has resulted in the past that it has now been agreed that the position of the movable object (boat) should be given as *from* the fixed object (rock). When, for example, the boat is west of the rock the bearing given should be 270°. But even if people are speaking the same language, and make every effort to be clear, misunderstandings still happen. I was at the helm of a boat entering a Californian marina. It was midweek and we were the only people sailing in the immediate area. Being unfamiliar with American buoys and signals, and seeing a buoy ahead in the middle of the channel, I said to the owner (who was originally English) 'Is that a middle ground buoy [which could be passed on either side] or is it a starboard hand buoy?' [meaning should I leave it on my right hand]. Relaxed, and with no problem in sight, he simply said the word 'Starboard'. This I took as affirmative to the second part of my question, and went to pass the left of the buoy. As we neared it, he woke up to the fact that we were going on the incorrect side – and he meant to go to starboard of it – but by then it was too late to divert. No harm was done, except that being an auxiliary coastguard he did not like his boat to be seen doing such unorthodox things. Faults on both sides, he should have answered my question fully, and when he did not, I should have rechecked the reply.

Peter Scott, the wildlife expert, was driving through narrow lanes near his home thinking about something else, when a car came round a bend towards him. Both cars braked and swerved, and as they passed extremely close, the woman driving the other car shouted at him 'pig'. Peter Scott was taken aback. He knew he had perhaps been a little slow in reacting, but there had not been any risk of an accident, and he felt that the comment was uncalled for. He drove on round the bend and there sitting in the middle of the lane was a vast pig.

Although chat on overcrowded radio frequencies needs to be kept to a minimum this can be overdone, as it is essential for enough information to be built into a message to avoid ambiguity. Two military pilots were taxiing out along the perimeter track one behind the other in their F84s when the second, seeing flames coming from the tail of his leader, called, 'Mike, you're on fire.' A moment later a pilot baled out of another F84 thousands of feet up and many miles away. He too was called Mike.

The main problem with simple communication errors of this sort is that the provider of the information or instruction does not appreciate that the person receiving the information could possibly get it wrong. Yet failed communication is Murphy's big success story. If a message can be given with ambiguity, or received incorrectly, it will be. If the message or instruction has to go through a third person, or be relayed in any way, the likelihood of change in meaning or emphasis will be more than doubled.

Even the Eyes Can Get it Wrong

Communication is not only a problem for the ears, but also for the eyes, though the increased use of visual symbols or colours has done much to reduce confusion. Red and blue on taps for example, are a distinct improvement on H (hot) and C (cold), chaud being French for hot, and caldo Italian. Hladan is cold in Serbo-Croat, and hideg in Hungarian. O and F on fuel gauges is better than E and F, but O to 4/4 is better still.

Nevertheless, visual confusions have turned up in quite unexpected ways. Over the last fifty years various so-called primitive tribes have been handed out so-called benefits of civilisation. One of these was food in cans – preserved, hygienic and easy to store. Cans showing appetising baked beans, steak and corn were readily eaten. But the tins of baby food were not touched, being discovered in heaps far outside the villages; their wrappers still showing fading pictures of happy, bouncing babies.

Remotely by Radio

If it is so easy to fail to get even simple messages across with any accuracy when there is direct face-to-face contact between people, then doing so remotely by radio provides even better opportunities for confusion. Not only is human mishearing, misinterpretation and misunderstanding of the information possible, but the equipment itself may work intermittently, too faintly, or not at all. As if these were not enough there is the problem of channels (frequencies). Although, for example, VHF will carry an enormous amount of traffic problems occur when users of a single frequency unexpectedly find themselves involved in someone else's activities, such as the organisers of a gliding championship in the north of England who were temporarily allocated a frequency to help with the retrieval of gliders from fields. Instructions to the trailer crews were picked up by Premix Concrete lorries, whose drivers became quite distracted. On another occasion a Securicor van driver was astonished to be informed over his radio that a motor cruiser was in distress from engine failure at sea and required assistance. He stopped, telephoned the coastguard, and the cruiser was eventually towed in by the lifeboat. The skipper who was a careful man, in spite of his engine failing, had recently sent his radio to the makers for servicing. The firm also serviced the Securicor radios, and had simply installed the wrong crystal.

Another problem was more difficult to solve. A nursing home for elderly male patients contained several who had been fitted with an electronic gadget which, when switched on, helped them empty their bladders. What mystified the doctors was when all the patients wanted to go at exactly the same moment. It is not known who was the Sherlock Holmes who discovered that this regimented behaviour coincided exactly with each sortie of the local lifeboat. They were using the same frequency.

Search and Rescue Problems

It is perhaps in search-and-rescue operations that communication problems can become most complicated. There may be difficulties in communication because there is no common radio frequency – even telephones sometimes have to provide the link. There can be language difficulties, and there can be confusion caused by well-meaning helpers who make unnecessary or wrong signals. Searches are frequently lengthened or made abortive by incorrect navigational or situation information being given; and some people, who have called for assistance and subsequently get themselves home, forgetting to cancel their cry of distress. Then there is the rescuer who, having effected a rescue, has no means of informing anyone that he has done so; in some cases he may not even know that a search is on.

There are, of course, considerable shortcomings in the radio communications end of the rescue services. Although co-ordination of the many facilities is carried out with great efficiency, it is still not possible for all the agencies to always talk to each other directly. Perhaps the least satisfactory aspect of this is that most aircraft, which are not only excellent observation platforms and by virtue of their altitude obtain enhanced VHF range, operate on a different range of frequencies from marine VHF and do not carry HF. An aircraft putting out a distress call does so on 121·5 MHz, and a boat on either 2182 kHz, or channel 16 (156·8 MHz). This means, immediately, that aeroplanes, unless specially equipped, remain unaware of problems on the water underneath them; and boats will not know of aeroplanes down in the drink. When the problem reaches the rescue co-ordination system a great deal of relaying of messages is necessary. However efficiently this is done, it cannot be as quick or as clear as if the helicopter could, for example, talk directly to the casualty, or to other units involved, such as the lifeboat or the mountain rescue team. In hilly areas, the helicopter may even be shielded by high ground to such an extent that it cannot talk to its own base. Delay in carrying out a rescue may in some cases be caused simply because the units have to get together before they set off, in order to make a plan and arrange signals. On one cliff-rescue where the coastguard on the cliff-top were out of sight and out of touch with their own people dealing with a severe injury under an overhang, the only means of communication was by transmission of hand signals from a helicopter hovering off the cliff-face and in sight of both parties.

There is a great need for a distress frequency common to all users – people at sea or in the air and rescuers – but it is not technically simple and its provision would be costly. This basic absence of a common distress call communication also exists with the various items of emergency beacon equipment, which is also carried over into unnecessary nomenclature confusion. If you fly you can carry an ELT (emergency location transmitter) or SARBE or EPIRB. In the event of a crash it is set off, or sets itself off, and transmits on 121·5 and probably the national military aviation frequency continuously for a period of x hours. The marine equivalent, such as the Callbuoy, transmits on 2182 kHz and probably 550 kHz, and may or may not have a direct talk capability. A pilot flying extensively over water might be advised to carry both, regardless of the extra cost.

Overcoming Deficiencies

In spite of all these deficiencies in rescue communications, people involved in rescue work become incredibly good in overcoming any communication problems that result. Early one morning the R.A.F. contacted the duty officer of the Army air squadron in Northern Ireland, and asked him to call the coastguard as he understood a trawler was being driven ashore in gale force winds. Two other trawlers were standing by, but the seas were too big for the lifeboat to be launched. The R.A.F. said they had already alerted the Irish Army Rescue centre who were sending a rescue helicopter. The Army air squadron duty officer, who was a light helicopter pilot, was to stand by.

Fifty minutes later the duty officer was told that the rescue helicopter could not be expected to arrive for 2 hrs, due to strong headwinds, and that he should fly to the scene to give any assistance that seemed possible. He did so, found the trawler lying in breaking seas about half a mile from the shore, so landed beside the local lighthouse station, which had radio-telephone contact with the trawler. This means of communication was valuable, though not very clear because the lighthouse used single side-band hf and the trawler, double side-band. The lack of clarity was not made easier by the mixture of Irish, Scots and English accents involved.

At 09.30 the rescue helicopter arrived and landed by the lighthouse, so that a plan could be made and given to the lighthouse keeper, who was the only radio contact with the casualty. The intention was for the rescue helicopter to take a light line from the distressed trawler to one of the other two standing by, who could then haul in a heavier line and tow off the grounded boat. The problem was that the line had to be very long, and the rescue helicopter did not have enough power to keep it stretched out

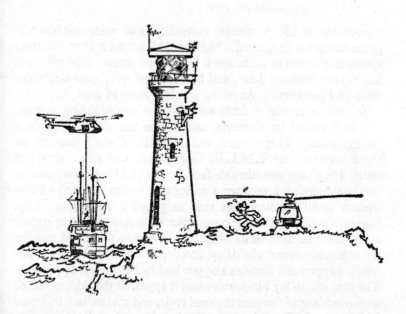

and every time it sagged into the sea it threatened to bring the rescue helicopter down with it. It was necessary for the trawler waiting to take the line to be manoeuvred with some precision to aid the rescue helicopter, and the only way for the necessary instructions to be passed was for the duty officer to run back and forth between his helicopter, which could talk to the other chopper, and the lighthouse, which could talk to the trawler. It worked, a towing line was tailed to the light line and hauled aboard, and the trawler successfully towed off by its mate.

Triggering the System

Some people seem to have the idea, when calling out rescue services, that a lifeboat, or helicopter complete with winchman, is something that they have some sort of right to. It is not often enough appreciated that the rescue service is complex and costly, because there is only one way to deal with search and rescue; and that is to have an organisation capable of dealing with almost any type of calamity, and able to remain operational until the rescue is completed, or called off because there is no longer reasonable expectation of life. It means, inevitably, that when the alarm is given this must trigger off a highly sophisticated system whatever doubt may be felt as to the need. Search and rescue, to be effective, has to start without delay, and be sustained with great determination and persistence. Anything less is a waste of time.

In Britain rescue is dealt with by two co-ordinating centres, one in Scotland (at Pitreavie) and one in the south of England (at Plymouth). They co-ordinate all facilities which include the three services, the R.N.L.I., Coastguard, and other specialist units. They have considerable facilities, but still have communication problems, such as when a coastguard station received a signal from a small Russian boat that they had a medical casualty. Pitreavie made ready a helicopter, but since it would be operating at the extreme limit of its range, it was essential it could pick up the sick man without any delay, and depart. To make sure that this would happen the Russian skipper had to be briefed in advance. The first stumbling block was when it appeared the skipper lacked understanding of the international code, and that no one on board had any useful English. Pitreavie then located an English coastguard who spoke Russian, but it was impossible to establish a link-call with the boat. Finally the Russian-speaking coastguard put instructions in the Russian language into the English alphabet, sent the message by teleprinter to Malin Head Coastguard Station, from where it was transmitted in morse code to the boat. It worked.

Sorting out the Situation

On another occasion a Dutch boat radioed the coastguard at Southend that they had picked up a lifebuoy and its flashing light, marked Pando. An hour earlier in the evening a tanker of that name had left Purfleet to dock up the river. A little later North Foreland radio reported that a British steamer had picked up a lifebuoy and float. This was marked P & O SNC. The British ship had made a search in the area, and found nothing else. The coastguard tried to discover if this second lifebuoy also had a flashing light and also if any P & O vessels had passed up or down the river recently; and if so had they lost a lifebuoy. They found that a P & O liner had passed outward at 19.00 hrs. Then the Pando came back to say she had not lost a lifebuoy, and in any case her lifebuoys did not have lights. During all this time a lifeboat had been kept at the ready. The coastguard then requested information as to whether the P & O liner had lost one of its lifebuoys on the way down-river. Nearly two hours elapsed before the message was answered. In the meantime the British steamer came back to say the lifebuoy she had picked up did have a light. The suspicion was now growing that the word Pando on the other buoy might have been a misreading of P and O by the Dutch crew. A radio call was put out to the Dutch ship to check this, but as time was passing a precautionary alert was broadcast to shipping, and as the two buoys had been picked up close to the same position the Southend lifeboat was launched to search this area. With, at this time, still no reply from the P & O liner, arrangements were made with another coastguard station to contact the liner as she passed their position, and also with the Dungeness pilot cutter to do the same thing. This at last produced news that the liner had lost two lifebuoys (but no persons), and that at least one of the buoys had been accidentally thrown overboard. It may have been a large ship but some of the people on her were no better at avoiding confusion than anyone else.

Almost all communication problems stem not from an ability to say something or send a message but from the failure to appreciate how others will react to the communication. In this last case the communication was a lifebuoy in the water and as such has both meaning and implication. It is Law to go to the aid of someone in distress at sea. Further, rescue services on receipt of reasonable evidence – such as a floating lifebuoy – have to react.

Finding the Casualty

Probably the most prevalent communication failure concerning rescue is that the position of the casualty is given incorrectly. As has already been mentioned most boats that go aground do so because they were not where they thought they were, but they SOS that position. Major searches have even been carried out on the north side of the very sizeable Cornish peninsula, near Padstow, when the boat was banging itself to pieces on the south side off the Lizard. The coastguard nearly goes crazy dealing with the whereabouts of people who fall over cliffs, when breathless friends call them with, 'He fell off the cliffs where they are rocky, please hurry.' At least in these incidents the coastguards know they are going to get inadequate information, they know what questions to ask quickly, and they also know their patch. More difficult to deal with is information that sounds precise and comes from what could be termed a reliable source.

Last year there was a yacht race in the Irish Sea in rough weather. Crews were tired, with the crew of the boat lying in third place nearing exhaustion. Not too surprisingly she ran aground in shoal water a few miles from land. The yacht in the lead saw the red distress flares, considered she was too far off to return so, having VHF radio, she called Rosslare that *a* boat was in distress, and gave the position. The yacht lying second turned back, but finding herself on the wrong side of the shoal on which the boat was now starting to break up could do nothing. However, a fourth boat was able to go in on the lee side of the shoal and with great skill took off the crew from their liferaft. The wrecked boat had no radio and neither did boats 2 and 4, and so no one was able to report that the survivors had been picked up; but equally, they were unaware that anyone else had put out a distress call. So boats 2 and 4 continued on their way.

In the meantime the Rosslare lifeboat searched the wrong part of the sea, not knowing that the lead boat had given a position no less than 18 miles adrift! It was not important that the skipper did not know either his or the casualties' exact position. What was important was that he should give only *true* information which would lead rescuers to the wrecked boat with the minimum delay. Instead of which, through ignorance, or pride, and above all no understanding of the probable reaction to his communication, he gave a precise position which was wrong. While the lifeboat continued searching in this area the rescue organisation became further confused when competitor No. 6, arrived near the shoal. He had radio and had heard the original call put out by the lead boat. Boat No. 6 properly started to search, and eventually located the wrecked boat. Being a conscientious seaman the skipper managed to put a man aboard in case the crew were still there, injured; but they found her deserted. They called Rosslare reporting what they had done, exactly where the wreck was, and the name of the yacht. Now the Arklow lifeboat was sent out to search this area for survivors since the rescue co-ordinators no longer could be certain that they had only a single casualty; and as long as any doubt remained that it might be more than one they had to work on this assumption. It would certainly not have been the first time that two, or even more, quite unrelated incidents had been reported in circumstances that could mislead into their being thought the same one. Since it is known that most people reporting sightings of flares or accidents do so with considerable lack of factual accuracy or observation, and that different reports of a single event will almost certainly vary, it is not difficult to assume in the first instance that this is the reason for any discrepancies in position or description. In fine weather it may even seem to be stretching the long arm of coincidence to expect more than one disaster in the same area at the same time. But it happens.

Stopping the Search

A great deal of communication confusion is caused by boats left adrift after the occupants have been taken off by a passing vessel. Later the abandoned boat is spotted by someone else who investigates, and discovers no one on board. If they have VHF they put out a call, and a search is started for people who may have fallen overboard. If the weather is wild, and the distressed boat is in a sinking state when left, it may be impossible or unnecessary to leave information as to action taken by the crew, but if the boat is likely to remain afloat, and cannot be taken in tow, then a note in a plastic bag should, if possible, be left aboard. Last year the occupant of a sailing dinghy became seasick and hailed a passing motor cruiser, owned by a friend, to take him aboard. Without further thought they all went home. Later the dinghy was seen and investigated after it had drifted several miles out to sea. It had one sail set, and there was a life-jacket, oars and other small possessions aboard. Since there was no communication in any form that the occupant was safe, it had to be assumed that he was not. Several thousand pounds of taxpayers' money evaporated in the search.

Attracting Attention

Another real problem in rescue communications is that of attracting attention, because until a casualty can be found, or is seen, he cannot be rescued. Whether it is a small dinghy or life-raft at sea, a climber who has fallen, or a small aeroplane in broken or wooded country does not matter; all will be difficult to see. At night it will be impossible – unless means of attracting attention are carried. Radio beacons for this purpose have been mentioned, but what has not been is the second-order problem that reduces the effectiveness of these admirable items: they go off when not intended to for various reasons. In 1975 the US Air Force Center logged 6,600 ELT activations, of which no less than 97 per cent were false alarms.* The main reasons were over-sensitive switches, so that they could easily be switched on by a weak, injured person, but they also could be set off by a heavy landing. The pilot might even be unaware that the set had been triggered, and lock up the aircraft in his hangar having failed to check the set before going home. ELTs have also gone off in the mail on their way back for servicing. They have also not activated when required through dud and corroded batteries, and through being mounted wrongly so that the g switch intended to operate in a crash deceleration would not work. Nevertheless, emergency radio beacons have resulted in hundreds of people staying alive who have crashed, fallen or sunk far beyond the range of possible rescue by visual signals.

For most activities the less expensive flare, or even the cheap torch, is enough to communicate the necessary request for aid. Yet people fly at night, become benighted on mountains, or drift about in dinghies without taking as an irreducible minimum, even a pocket flashlight with a good battery. One evening at 20.40 a woman telephoned the Bangor rescue headquarters in Northern Ireland to say that her husband and two friends had not returned from fishing in their 12-ft dinghy. Since the wind was now force 8, gusting 9, from WSW, a night search was immediately started by the lifeboat assisted by two fishing boats. The Co. Down coast was also searched by the coastguard, but with no success. At first light

* In Britain 98 per cent of burglar alarm triggerings are false.

a helicopter from Aldergrove, Northern Ireland, took off to look, and the Scottish Coastguard started to search the enormously lengthy and indented shores of Wigtown. The dinghy, equipped with only one life-jacket, and having lost an oar, hit Scotland before dawn, drowning two men in the rocky surf. The third, an ex-paratrooper PT instructor, managed to reach shore and climb the cliffs. During the night drift across the North Irish Sea they had seen several boats pass close to the dinghy on both sides, but they had no means of attracting attention. Even daylight pilots who do the searching say that a Nimrod needs 9 hrs to thoroughly inspect an area 30 × 30 miles in rough weather, and that from a helicopter a person in even small waves cannot be seen with any certainty above 100 ft.

A situation which repeats itself with depressing frequency is the small dinghy sinking on its return to the bigger boat out on moorings. These dramas usually take place after dark (after the pubs close), there are often too many people in the dinghy (to save a second journey) so the freeboard is minimal, and often the wind or the tide is more troublesome than it had been earlier. So the dinghy submerges or capsizes, and people become drowned, or are found quite by chance hanging on to an anchor rope of their own or someone else's boat. These accidents invariably occur in harbours, or other waters where there are plenty of other people around to help – except that they cannot see wet heads bobbing about in dark water. Yet even a 4-in.-long plastic pocket flashlight, wrapped with watertight PVC tape, could be enough in these circumstances to result in rescue. Attracting attention should be regarded simply as a means of communication – no more, no less. Instead too many people look on flares, pocket strobe lights, or serviceable flashlights, as bothersome emergency equipment, to care for the accident that is not going to happen to them.

Communication, in the sense of attracting attention, is also sometimes unnecessarily non-existent because of shortage of intelligent thought; like the bright red and yellow high-visibility aeroplane that force-landed in the snowy Labrador tundra, and turned, quite gently, upside down. The undersurfaces were all painted white. Among the passengers were some Eskimos who promptly made an efficient but invisible white snow igloo, in which everyone sat, eating their emergency rations and wondering why no one found them. They had, of course, several communication possibilities, ranging from making a fire (searches begin at the upwind end of smoke), flashing with a mirror or piece of polished steel, or aluminium, and treading down an SOS or pattern of straight lines on the ground. The snow, brush, sand, or whatever, should be banked along one edge of the lines, because it is the shadow in the low sun of morning and evening which makes this type of signal very clear.

Transposition Errors and Misinterpretations

This chapter has described many ways in which communications can fail between people, but it is also possible to have communication failures with oneself, when, for example, one reads a telephone number from the directory, and the brain instructs the finger to dial something else. Such transposition errors are not uncommon, but like many human failures are made worse by fatigue or stress. It is probably in flying that transposition errors are most common, for the simple reason that a large number of instrument readings and adjustments are necessary. One airline pilot set his altimeter sub-scale to 938 mb instead of 839 mb, and touched ground 9 miles short of the runway. Close to the transposition error is the misinterpretation error. One light aeroplane pilot spun in because he failed to appreciate that the ASI of this particular French aeroplane was in km/h and not mph, and he flew it too slowly. Another pilot, lost above cloud as a result of an initial and fundamental navigational error, homed on an oil-rig beacon, on 325 kHz, instead of the Newcastle beacon, given him by air traffic control. This was also on 325 kHz but the difference in compass heading was more than 90°. He was finally identified by radar over the North Sea nearly 100 miles NNE of Aberdeen and about 210 nautical miles from where he thought he was. He then did not have enough fuel to get back to land, and although an R.A.F. search Nimrod laid a flare path on the sea for him, the waves were too big and he did not make it.

Misinterpretation errors are very easy to make. I flew a little aeroplane once which showed 4,000 revs, or 40 for short, on the rev counter at full throttle. Next to this instrument was the airspeed indicator. The correct climb speed was 40 knots. The first time I flew the aeroplane I thought I was flying with great precision during the climb-out as the needle did not flicker from 40. It was the wrong needle. Errors of this sort are easy to come by in boats by switching the echo-sounder by mistake to feet instead of fathoms, or misreading aircraft altimeters because some are in feet and others in metres, or misreading diving decompression tables. Because of the ease and frequency with which such mistakes can be made, every reading or interpretation of importance should be cross-checked as far as possible by common sense. A pilot flying a strange aeroplane should back up the airspeed reading by checking on the handling and feel of the controls. Little aeroplanes are not so sophisticated that the controls do not begin to feel sloppy or the aircraft develop a sinking feeling when flown on the slow side. Compass readings in boats should be checked against the position of the sun, or even a steady wind direction, to minimise errors. The 'black on red' syndrome, flying 180° wrong, is a perennial.

Equipment Communications

There is one more aspect of communications which, when it is non-existent or fails, results in accidents which are quite unnecessary. As equipment becomes more sophisticated it will not only contain more elements which can go wrong, but an increasing number of failures will not be able to be repaired by someone on the spot. It was said that the Peninsular War was won because the British horse harness was designed to be repaired by rope, and the French harness was irreparable in the field. Whether this was true or not, the fact is that if equipment cannot be quickly and simply mended, then it is essential that all users of this equipment know, or are kept informed of, what faults are likely to develop.

It is only very recently that an international system of air transport hazard reporting has been agreed. And although this is probably more fundamental on large airliners than anything else, it may still be a life-saver to the balloon or hang glider pilot, the diver or the mountaineer. It is an aspect of communication for which every user of equipment has a responsibility.

If a new boat develops weakness in the rudder fittings, the manufacturer should be told; if a glider pilot finds it is possible to rig his aircraft wrongly in an unexpected way he should tell the manufacturer, and his national association, so that information can be given to others as quickly as possible. One person bought a small cabin heater for his boat which had a plastic casing. It was thought to be impossible for this stove to set itself on fire, but when it did, the plastic melted and set fire to other things as well. The letter the owner wrote to a sailing magazine was quickly published.

Good communications is primarily a matter of common sense, and more than anything an ability to understand what will be the effect of the message on the recipient, who may not have the background or any other information possessed by the sender. Which reminds me of a friend who spent a happy time on a beach, sending off a message in a bottle, which he knew would come ashore about 200 yds away. He watched through binoculars, fascinated at the reaction of the holiday-makers to his note in English purporting to come from a sinking Russian submarine under the Arctic ice!

9 ◇ COMPETENCE AND ANTICIPATION

If accidents are caused by the failings of poor teaching or communication, carelessness, mismanagement, irresponsibility or incompetence, it may be equally said that they are avoided by the
converse – good management, responsibility and competence.
This is certainly so, and it may be worth looking at what actually
makes up those qualities and skills that keep so many people
remarkably free of disaster. It may be said that someone is a good
driver or a good pilot, but attempts are seldom made to analyse
what are the ingredients that make him good. If proper management is necessary to conduct an expedition, however small,
efficiently and safely, what actually goes to make up a good
manager? Probably the first essential is skill, the ability to do
something accurately and correctly. If the skill is not there no
amount of other good qualities will make up for its absence. If,
for example, a person cannot handle a boat with reasonable
accuracy on all points of sailing, navigate it to where he intends
to go and get back again, anchor or moor it safely, and leave
it in good condition, then he cannot call himself a sailor; and he
should not embark upon the waters other than in a learning
capacity.

Gaining Experience

Experience is skill consolidated and broadened. Some people
seem to believe that if they have held a pilot licence for 5 years, or
have now got 2 years' worth of dives in their log-book, they are
automatically experienced. But gaining experience is not merely
going on doing something; it means continually improving the
standard of attainment, and working at adding further contributory skills. There is a tendency today to specialise in almost everything. It starts in secondary schools, it continues with courses in

hill walking, gliding, advanced canoeing, and it is deeply built in to industry. It becomes very easy for a person to believe that what he is taught is all that he needs to know, and that knowing it means that he is skilled. Other things are for other people – knowledge of the bends for divers, knots for scouts, or thermals for glider pilots. But broadening of experience means breaking out of such a narrow and limited framework and developing it as far as possible. For a start everyone involved in any open-ended activity, such as flying in any form, or mountaineering or diving, needs to have a real understanding of the weather if he is to be able to fully use his skill. And it is not only boy scouts and sailors who need to know how to tie a knot; more than one pilot has lost £20,000 of aeroplane in the night because he was incompetent in securing his picket ropes, and an unexpected gale blew the aircraft over. The glider pilot needs to know from the air what field crops look like if he is not to put himself out of a competition by ground-looping in kale, the diver needs to know how to use a compass, and everyone needs to understand the technicalities of their equipment. Experience means knowing that wheels clogged with slush will freeze solid in the air and not rotate on landing; that it is easy to become disorientated under water but to find which way is up by watching breath bubbles; that if field landing a glider telephone or power wires should be expected along any hedge bordering a road; and that outboard engines should be expected to oil up their plugs if run slowly for any length of time.

Anticipation and Observation

Two valuable attributes which are a powerful force in the avoidance of accidents are a sense of anticipation and good observation. Anticipation is the ability to use the imagination to study what is likely to happen, or what could go wrong. The glider pilot who anticipates that the launch cable may break will be less surprised and better prepared to act when it does. The climber, who anticipates falling stones, will not leave his helmet at home. Some people develop their sense of anticipation to an uncanny extent, and always seem somehow to be in the right place at the right time, like being snugly in harbour when there is an 'unexpected' gale, or over good open country when the aeroplane engine fails. Not long ago a navy jet pilot about to be catapulted from a carrier signalled 'Ready'. The catapult fired accelerating the jet from 0 to 90 knots in 3 sec, and as it went a piece of metal flew into the engine intake producing total loss of power on that engine. Five seconds from giving the signal to go the pilot's feet touched the sea. In those 5 sec he had appreciated the problem, taken the decision to eject, and ejected with the parachute deploying enough to enable him to arrive feet first in the ocean. The pilot had never ejected before, but early in his training he had anticipated that one day he might have to use his chute, and that the time available for thought would be minimal. Several years passed, but during all this time he touched and confirmed the location of the eject handle before each take-off and mentally prepared himself. When it finally happened all he needed to stay alive was the minimum physical reaction time.

Anticipation is helped by good observation, which may have nothing to do with good eyesight. Good observation is the ability of the brain to be curious about what the eye sees, and to register this curiosity. It is the ability to see and recognise what is being looked at, or for. It is, for example, good observation that will pick up the *first* sign of changing weather so that the brain can get to work on possible alternative plans.

One bright cold winter day a pilot was happily making a flight along the coast. At about 50 miles from home, where he was going to turn round anyway, there was an old deserted airfield right by the beach. The runway looked sound enough for landing, there was a windsock and he felt it would be fun to walk along the beach to look at the waves and flakes of sea ice from close to. Being a careful sort of person he called his base on the radio, told them his intentions and said he would call again as soon as he was once more airborne, in maximum 40 min time.

He then checked on the windsock and came into land. But something seemed wrong, his slow little aeroplane was using up the runway like a jet fighter. He checked his approach speed, which was about right, so opened up and went round again to have another try. The windsock still showed plenty of wind, he approached as slowly as he dared, but the same thing happened. Puzzled, but determined not to be done out of his stroll on the beach, he came in a third time, as low, slow, and short over the

runway threshold as he could. He made it, just, and taxied over to what had originally been the aircraft park, and got out. Still puzzled, he looked up at the windsock, and felt the cold wind on his face – from the other direction. The windsock was frozen stiff, mutely pointing the wrong way. But there had been so many other signs he had not observed. The direction of the movements of the white wave caps, wind ripples on the water, seagulls taking off, and even the little clouds blowing across the sky trailing their shadows. Convinced that the windsock would provide the information, he had not observed anything else at all. Not even when he realised that something odd was happening.

Concentrating the Mind

High on the list of valuable attributes is thoroughness, particularly in preparation. It is no good being an excellent navigator if the charts have been left at home, and even more useless doing a pre-flight inspection on an aircraft if faults are missed. The ability to be thorough requires knowledge of the subject, a mind which can be concentrated, and patience; and it needs to be a habit, not merely produced only when life obviously depends upon it. Qualities that make up thoroughness were shown by Llewelyn in the 1930s during a flight he made from London to Johannesburg in a tiny Aeronca powered by a 36 hp twin-cylinder JAP engine. To improve the engine performance for subsequent flying in Johannesburg, 5,000 ft up, after his arrival, he had taken along with him a pair of high-compression pistons. On the way, over Kenya, he was beset by violent thunderstorms. He landed in a clearing in the bush to wait until they had dispersed and it was safe to continue, but far from any habitation or sign of life. While waiting for the weather he measured the take-off length available, considered the altitude of the clearing and the air temperature, and concluded that he would not be able to clear the trees at the end unless he fitted his high-compression pistons. So he set to work, dismantled the engine, changed the pistons; and then decided it necessary to grind in the valves. It was while replacing them that one of the small split valve cotters went 'ping' and vanished. Realising that unless he could find it his chance of survival was very small, he drew a series of concentric circles in the dirt around the nose of the aeroplane and started a systematic search. After 11 hrs he found it, assembled the engine, took off safely and flew on to civilisation.

The Honesty Problem

Honesty, or the avoidance of deceiving oneself, is another attribute that makes for safer operations; map reading being one of the easiest ways a person has of persuading himself that something is right when it is not. People who convince themselves that the bad weather will not come their way are as plentiful as the raindrops themselves. A more difficult honesty problem sometimes occurs when doing a pre-flight inspection on a light aeroplane or glider. It is easy to say that no aircraft should be flown unless it is absolutely right, but no aircraft is perfect, and neither is anything else. The fault may be something vital. That makes it easy; the aircraft is unserviceable and cannot be flown. More likely it will be something minor which could not be expected to affect its safe operation. The honesty problem is at its most difficult when the courses of action are limited. The pilot can either decide on his own knowledge and responsibility that the aircraft is safe to fly – which means that he has to be very honest in the assessment of his own ability – or he can put the aircraft unserviceable, perhaps unnecessarily. Alternatively, he hands the decision and the responsibility over to someone else – who he may know to be less skilled or able. The problem of slightly unserviceable and hard-worked school aircraft is an everyday one for an instructor, and is a situation in which he has to be absolutely honest with himself. Whether he puts the aircraft serviceable or not must be on grounds of safety; not expediency, or convenience, or pride, or 'Daddy knows best'.

Ingenuity

In addition to all the other qualities, the possession of ingenuity is an asset. So often, in any sort of problem, the best answer does not come into the mind until too late – or at all. A quick and simple solution has been available, yet in the heat of the moment it did not present itself. One night during the Second World War a bomber crashlanded wheels-up in a muddy field with the front gunner trapped. The crew were desperately trying to lever up the massive fuselage enough to get him out, but were having no success. At that moment a small Dutch girl said in halting English 'Why not dig a hole?' She had even brought a spade.

A pilot bringing an Airacobra in to land could not get any indication that the nosewheel had come down. To land with it up or unlocked would have resulted in a 90 mph somersault. The emergency lowering system had been used without avail, and the air-craft had no radio to ask for a sighting by airfield staff, so the pilot banked the aircraft and flew it very low over open fields so that its shadow showed the position of the wheels. The nosewheel

was correctly positioned forward of the vertical, and so must have reached the locked-down position.

More recently a woman was trapped in her overturned car by her seat belt, which had become jammed. In a remote area and with the temperature below freezing she could not wait for help to come. She had no knife but remembered that there was a throw-away cigarette lighter in the glove pocket. She managed to extract it and tried to burn through the webbing. The fuel ran out before she had succeeded but the remaining strands had been weakened enough to be worried apart. Another person trapped in his overturned car for several days used electric flex from behind the instrument panel to lower his shirt into a stream below the car to sop up water to drink.

Coming to the Wrong Conclusions

The converse of ingenuity is leaping to the wrong conclusion, such as the sailor who having set off to cross the Atlantic one morning discovered quite a lot of water in the bilges. There had been a bit of a storm the night before, but the amount of water was more than would be expected. Being a well-equipped boat, with good pumps the water was soon returned to the sea. Only too late did the sailor discover that it was not the sea that had been leaking in but his precious drinking water that had been leaking out, and was now lost forever.

In 1919 Harry Hawker and Mackenzie-Grieve set out on what was to be the first non-stop crossing of the Atlantic – a month before Alcock and Brown. On the way across the engine overheated, so the controls were adjusted, but the overheating continued, and eventually with a seized engine Hawker had to ditch and await rescue. Only afterwards did he discover that the heat control had been mistakenly reconnected up the opposite way round. Every time he moved it he was contributing to the problem. To expect the expected is not an unusual human reaction – I once flew an aeroplane which required two hands on the stick to keep it flying level. I assumed the trouble was that the aeroplane was not in good condition, was of a type new to me, and because of the very turbulent air. Not once did the real reason occur to me – that the spring elevator trimmer could have been connected the wrong way round.

Visualising the Scene Again

Ingenuity is inborn in some people, but whether it is possessed or not, perhaps the best way of avoiding unnecessary accidents is to spend thinking time – one's bath is a good place – in 'visualising the scene'; in doing a sort of anticipation exercise. Remember the skipper, in an earlier chapter, who unexpectedly simulated a man-overboard situation, and was met with instant chaos? The sudden or unexpected emergency is best dealt with by considering well ahead of time the problems that might one day turn up, and in peace and quiet working out possible solutions. It is easy to assume, for example, that the main difficulty if a crewman goes overboard is manoeuvring into a position and speed to be able to pick him up. Not so; the big difficulty is usually physically getting him back on board.

As a diver. Say you were in charge of a sub-aqua club inflatable at sea on a fine day with two pairs of divers down in shallow (20–

30 ft) of water. Two divers return in good time and clamber aboard. There is then a pause and one diver of the second pair surfaces saying he can't find his buddy. You are in charge; what do you do? The diver on the bottom is likely to have somewhere between 5 and 15 min air left, and this does not allow you to waste any time at all on wondering whether you should go and get help. You are on your own. If you have already thought around this sort of problem you will probably get the single diver and the more experienced of the two who have surfaced to go down as a pair using whichever two bottles contain the most remaining air, and you will probably put the remaining diver in the water without a bottle to use his snorkel and observe as much as he can through his mask, and be prepared to go to the rescue.

You would watch the sea around for bubbles, having made a check on the time the rescue dive started. If the two that have gone down find the missing diver and lead him, or help him, or drag him to the surface, the snorkeler is in the best position to help, and so can you from the boat. If they return without him and there is no more air, all three should snorkel on a designated search area down tide of the boat until there is no possibility of the missing diver having any more air, plus 15 or 20 min. Until this time the boat should not be moved. When it is decided that the diver if still on the bottom must be dead, the position should be marked with a buoy or plastic container, and the inflatable taken *at least* a mile down tide with everyone on watch before returning home, and rescue services called out. The use of diver marker buoys will obviously minimise this sort of problem.

As a glider pilot. What would you do if at the top of a winch launch in a glider the cable would not release from the aircraft? You know it *must* release because it has safety devices, but this time it is stuck and you have to accept it; but you know that the winchman has means of cutting the cable at his end, so you wait for the freeing jerk but it doesn't come: instead the nose of the glider is being pulled steadily down, and speed is beginning to pick up. No amount of yanking back on the stick helps. You have something like 20 sec to make up your mind. I have been an onlooker to just such an incident. The first thing is to stop pulling the stick back, but push it forward and dive the glider to get some slack in the cable; then to pull the nose up suddenly and hope that the cable will break – the weak link being designed to fail before the glider. If this is not successful there is only one possible course left; to fly in descending circles around the winch endeavouring to build slack in the cable, hope it will not catch on obstructions, and land close to the winch. This has been done successfully, and with only minor damage to the glider, on at least two occasions. But it needs to be thought about first.

Sometimes the accident may be someone else's, but you are the only available aid. If you are with a friend in the mountains climbing, hang gliding, or just hill walking, and he falls, crashes, or slips, coming to rest on some ledge or outcrop below, which is completely inaccessible to you, the only thing to do is to get help quickly. But it will not help if you are unable to tell rescuers where to go. The problem may be simple because you are standing right beside a 100 per cent identifiable object, like a survey bench mark, but it is much more likely that you are just on a large chunk of hill or mountain, and do not even know your own position with the precision needed to accurately direct rescuers.

Anticipation Homework

This is part of the involvement in any of the more interesting activities in life, even though much of it is more mundane than the examples above. For *every* flight some anticipation homework should have been done, not only about things that were covered in training, such as when to deploy the reserve parachute, but about alternative plans and diversions in case the weather does not turn out as forecast, or the radio goes on the blink, or the engine fires intermittently but does not actually stop. It is a matter of thinking about critical actions that may become necessary, and the critical decisions needed to bring about the best retrieval of a situation in the often minimal time.

On reading accident reports it is perhaps the absence of any anticipation homework that stands out most clearly as an accident cause. So many of the unexpected things that happen could and should have been anticipated and thought about. Sometimes the effect of being caught unawares is total – as in the case of the couple whose motor boat caught fire while they were refuelling;

immediately they threw the remainder of the open can of fuel into the sea, and then jumped in after it. They were utterly astonished, though fortunately not badly burned, when the sea caught fire around them.

It is fairly easy today to fail to think either much or deeply about what one is doing – there is so much that imposes upon available time, courses of learning are offered with the attraction of limited commitment in time and money, and equipment from sophisticated aeroplanes to single-cell plastic inflatable boats is easily available – and invariably on credit. And people are labelled – he is a pilot, a flier, a parachutist, as though the title itself imbues the person with instant skill. But reality is not this at all. To sail or race a dinghy well and safely in all sorts of conditions takes time, effort, money, and thought. To fly a glider and obtain the immense satisfaction from using the energy of the air to soar demands not only hard work but probably considerable changes in the way one has always gone about things. Otherwise, the usual unimportant failings like complacency and carelessness result simply in the pilot failing to reach his objective. Further little faults like over-confidence or pride mean that he probably breaks the aircraft too. Mistakes are easy to make, and they will go on being made for every reason under the sun. They can be reduced by care and attention, and their effects minimised by thought and skill, but 'pilot error' in one of its many camouflages is likely to remain the most fruitful source of accidents in whatever we do. As a flying instructor once said of a pilot he had just tested, 'He carried out all the pre-flight checks and starting procedures faultlessly. His taxiing was careful and beyond reproach in all respects. On reaching the take-off point he completed the pre-take-off drills with deliberation and thoroughness. He then turned the aircraft into wind and opened the throttle thereby releasing forces over which he had no further control.'

Competence is a Quiet Quality

Drama is avoided because skill, modest self-reliance and experience have merged into the ability to manage and control whatever situations that befall.

Crossing the Atlantic in his 47-ft junk-rigged boat Jock McLeod had a university student hitch-hiker as his only crew. About half-way across to Ireland they hit the tail of a tropical storm, and in-spite of heaving-to were knocked down by the enormous seas. The battering went on for two days without any chance of establishing their position, and in the words of the skipper:

That evening we were engulfed once more by a breaking wave and knocked over. In the split second before it happened I recognised the same feeling and motion as before and was ready for it when it came. The same thing happened. We were smothered in foam and the light went green as we fell over. We both cried 'Oh no! not again!' This time only a few objects shifted from their stowage. A check from the hatch showed that all was still well on deck. I was a bit more apprehensive now and began to wonder if I was using the correct tactics for the conditions. Were two knockdowns in six hours an indication that I was doing the wrong thing? Was I asking too much of the boat or was it simply me that was weakening too soon? We were lying ahull but making some forward way. I presumed we were making a little easting but if I took down the foresail we would drift to the west of south. Did our slow forward movement aggravate the situation? I would like to have a really experienced [!] seaman on board to discuss the matter with. I was loath to turn and run under bare poles with the possible need to stream warps to slow us down and reduce the danger of being pooped; the nervous strain on the helmsman is considerable in these conditions as he tries to keep the stern into the seas, and with night approaching the difficulty of seeing the seas before they reached the boat would increase the chance of broaching by taking the sea too much on the quarter, and a broach could be just as bad, if not worse, than the knockdowns we had experienced. I decided to leave things as they were but there was still some doubt in my mind. I sought solace in the now rising barometer and my belief that the boat was well found and would look after us.

The conditions remained the same through the second dark night, but we had no more knockdowns. I found it difficult to relax completely but we both managed to have a reasonable sleep. By 07.00 the next morning the glass had risen considerably and was 10 millibars higher than its trough, and I confirmed my wishful thinking that the wind and sea were slowly moderating though it was very marginal at first. By noon I decided that the moderation was continuing fast and we could consider setting more sail, so we both dressed up in oilskins and harness and rigged a jury topping lift to replace the broken one. That afternoon the wind started to veer, which puzzled me a bit as it was not in accordance with what I imagined the weather pattern to be. The forecasts from St John's, which I had managed partially to get, were read out too fast and were too indistinct to be fully understood. The wind continued to veer and moderate, and the sea decreased too, though a slight cross-sea made us slam occasionally. We raised more sail and tacked to make up NE on a better course for Oban, though I had no clear idea of where we were. The only RDF station I had been able to get appeared to be in New Zealand! There was no chance of a sun sight that day. We had a good supper and got the BBC news on 1500 metres. The cloud cover became patchy the next morning and I was able to get some quick shots of the sun for the first time for three days. When we worked out the first one it put us well to the north of my dead reckoning position and I was very suspicious. I presumed that I had not used the true horizon but the top of a nearer sea instead. However, subsequent sights confirmed that we had indeed made about 120 miles on course for Oban, which must have been due to a tremendous push from the Gulf Stream more than compensating for leeway. This discovery really raised our morale.

PART TWO

✧ Equipment

10 ◇ EQUIPMENT DESIGN

Whether a person creates disaster as a result of his own errors, or avoids it by common sense and competence – and there are many people who do – he will still have to be prepared to cope with faulty equipment. It may be a simple item like a small rowing boat, or extremely complex like a fully instrumented aeroplane; but whatever it is it will sooner or later fail the user in some way. If this failure coincides with, or is added to, some personalised confusion then the accident moves nearer.

Some equipment has been developed over a very long period, e.g. sailing boats, or with remarkable speed over the last few years, e.g. hang gliders, but whichever it is there are pressures on the manufacturer who will not stay in business if he does not sell his goods. He has to produce what the customer wants to buy, and although in most sports equipment this is for goods of reliable quality there is also demand for more and better performance. People like to own something faster, newer, or more sophisticated than that possessed by their fellows; or they simply want to win.

Sometimes there is a reaction to the inevitable complexity to which 'progress' of this sort leads. The explosive growth of simple hang gliding was a reaction to the over-sophistication, over-regulation and high cost of conventional aviation. But hang gliding is already finding itself subject to just the same pressures. Higher-performance hang gliders are demanded, almost regardless of whether there has been *time* to find out with any certainty that they are suitable for use by the ordinary semi-skilled customer. Although hang gliding is an easy example to use, it is by no means the only one in which the rush and hurry to produce something 'better', together with the polarised objective of higher performance, has led to equipment which is not always as practical and safe as it might be. Ergonomics, the apparently simple science of designing equipment to fit the human user, is mainly thought about only when it is absent. This does not necessarily mean that solutions to ergonomic problems are not known; they are more likely not to have been applied. For example, there can be few people who have used the standard design of tin snips without getting a blood blister on the palm of their hands. One of the classic ergonomic bad designs was the traditional cork lifebelt with which every ship was liberally supplied. They may well have kept the mariner from sinking when in the water, but for people having to jump into the sea from a doomed ship they were guaranteed to render the survivor unconscious and speed him to his untimely end. On hitting the water the lifebelt delivered a knock-out blow to the jaw.

Ergonomic Problems

With the plethora of sports equipment now available the application of sound ergonomic principles in its design is important because of the extent to which the equipment is depended upon. It is essential that the webbing of a diver's weightbelt will not 'creep' when under water, because if it falls off inadvertently he will shoot to the surface and maybe damage his lungs. It is essential that the seat of a glider is comfortable because if it cramps and fatigues the pilot he will be more likely to break the aircraft at the end of an 8-hr flight, and it is essential that the rudder fittings on a boat match the strength of the boat itself –

they seldom do – because their failure can lose the whole boat and possibly its crew.

The ergonomic problem is twofold. To ensure that the equipment is properly designed in an engineering sense, so that it will not fail in normal use, and to ensure that it is suited in all respects to the human operator. This includes considerations of shape and other physical characteristics, such as strength, as well as the human capability of using it incorrectly, not even when aided by Murphy. In this respect the filler orifices for fuel and water seen on some cruising boats are a typical example. The orifices are positioned near each other on the deck, but with the titles 'fuel' and 'water' moulded into identically fitting filler *caps*, instead of on the necks of the orifices. It matters not that the owner knows his own boat and would never put the wrong liquid into the wrong holes. After lending his boat to a friend for a week one owner discovered to his horror that he had just boiled a kettle of petrol to shave with!

Suitability for the human operator is a more complex matter. People not only need different shaped seats, as they have long or short legs, but they may well use the equipment in a way that was not intended, or simply make any of a number of simple errors with it. If the equipment is straightforward, like a small sailing dinghy, this is where the reason for any problem ends. But a new difficulty arises if the equipment is highly sophisticated. It is not that it is too difficult for an intelligent or trained person to use, but that he needs to do so with considerable regularity – to keep in practice – if he is to continue to remain competent to operate it properly. With a bicycle, a small boat, or fins, mask and snorkel, it is not important if even several years elapse between sorties, the original skill returns almost at once. In diving, and especially flying, with its mixture of complex equipment and without easy means of rescue, the disadvantage of lay-off and becoming out of practice are much greater. But most people involve themselves in flying or other sports for recreation, in their spare time, and using their own money. The situation therefore exists, notwithstanding any operator licence-renewal requirements, that once equipment has reached a certain degree of complexity, the chances of its misoperation are increased; often by those very people who do not wish to make mistakes. It is in this area that good ergonomic solutions are most needed, because people do not just stop doing those things on which they have set their heart because other people get killed or injured.

Why No Fuel?

It is probably in aeroplane fuel systems and controls that the ergonomic problem moves towards the shambolic. Pilots are just as capable of running out of petrol as are motorists; they can switch to a wrong tank in a moment of aberration, and they can fail to check that their tanks do not contain condensation water as well as petrol, or even anything at all. But accidents from these causes constitute only about half of the total accidents resulting from fuel failure. The others are caused by bad design, unnecessary complication, poor presentation of information, and maintenance failures, some of which are due to poor design. On some systems the fuel tank indicator is in the form of a circular plate marked into a number of segments indicating off, left, right, and both tanks. Pivoting on this plate is a lever swinging around its centre. One end of the lever is the pointer, to be aimed at the appropriate tank position, and the other end is the handle by which the pointer is positioned. This design, which has been around for a long time, fails because (a) it is easy to confuse the pointer and the handle, particularly for an inexperienced pilot trying to remember a lot of new things at the same time – not even one end of the lever is painted differently from the other; (b) it is possible to position the pointer between tanks; and (c) if maintenance is not all that good the indication plate itself may slip around so that the pointer indication is unknown.

Another type of fuel gauge is similar to that on many cars; a needle swinging between E for empty on the left and F for full on the right. In between are division marks numbered in gallons. One knows from automobile experience that fuel gauges are not always all that accurate, and not only because there may be some water in the bottom of the tank, yet the division space between empty and 5 gallons on one such aeroplane gauge is a bare $\frac{1}{8}$ in. with the needle width only fractionally less; 5 gallons for this engine is almost one hour's flying at normal cruise. But even if the pilot plays safe and reckons on landing within 20 min of the gauge starting to indicate 5 gallons, he may still be caught out.

Yet another fuel gauge consists of a transparent tube under a transparent panel in each wing root, directly connected to each fuel tank in each wing. As the fuel is consumed so the amount can be seen to drop in the transparent tube. Foolproof? Not always, because on some aircraft both the tops and bottoms of the tubes are hidden by the surround of the transparent panel; so if the fuel is colourless it is not always possible to tell if the tank is completely full or completely empty, because no fuel *level* is visible. It is easy to say the pilot should have checked, and so he should. Failure to do so by actually dipping the tank, as well as by looking at the gauge, may be due to the pilot taking over from another who says the aeroplane has plenty of fuel, or leaving the aircraft to be refuelled and this is not done. On both occasions a pilot not familiar with this type of fuel gauge may perhaps be forgiven when his visual check appears to indicate that a tank is completely full. But whether the pilot has, or has not, been insufficiently thorough, it is not necessary to add to his workload by difficulty in the operation of the equipment.

Why Engines Stop

Next in the fuel variety bill is the positioning of the fuel cock itself. It was only after a couple of fatal accidents on an otherwise excellent and well-made, small twin-engined aircraft that it was discovered that it was possible for passengers in the rear seats to inadvertently kick not one, but *both* fuel selectors into an intermediate position so that they provided no further fuel. On a two-seat motor glider used for elementary pilot training the authorities decided that the fuel cock in the cockpit constituted a break in the fuel line at which a leak might occur, so on subsequent models they required the cock to be changed to a position at the rear of the cabin on the luggage shelf, with the joint outside the cabin wall. It certainly obviated the possible leak – which had never been known to occur, but instead created a situation in which the instructor could not see or reach the cock in flight or turn it off in the event of a forced landing, but in which the fuel could accidentally be turned off in the air by a passenger pulling, say, a camera from the shelf, if the strap caught around the cock handle.

It would take far too many pages to cover even briefly the wide varieties of not altogether satisfactory fuel and cross-feed systems that are flying around, but as an example there is an aircraft which will drain petrol from the main to the auxiliary tank if the fuel is not turned off on the ground; on this aircraft take-off is made using the main tank, but on other aircraft take-off has to be made on a header tank before switching to main. Then there is the question of checking for water in the fuel before take-off, usually by pushing up on a little spring plunger in the bottom of the tank under the wing. Some designs of plunger return automatically when the finger is removed, and others can be made to stay open by giving the plunger a half-turn. If this is not appreciated it is easy to inadvertently impart a slight twist when checking for water and so unknowingly leave the drain slightly open. In flight it will do as drains do. Extra care has to be taken when checking the water in helicopter tanks. Unlike aeroplanes which are usually parked on level ground, helicopters may be sitting on a slope so that the drain plug is no longer at the lowest point, but the water is; though this is more of a pilot appreciation problem than a design one.

Controls, Instruments and Seats

Other design inadequacies in aircraft include aeroplanes of the same sort being fitted with flap selector switches of different types. On one the flaps will remain in whatever position they are at when the lever is released; on the other they return all the way up. Since at a slow speed instant removal of all flap can dump the aircraft abruptly on to the ground, the result may be expensive. There are pairs of rudder pedals in side-by-side seated aircraft in which the pedals are so close, and feel so similar that pilots have taken off using two left pedals, one foot on their own and the other on the passenger's. There are airspeed static pressure selectors fitted under the instrument panel and so adjacent to the cabin heat controls, that one pilot, thinking he was fumbling with the latter inadvertently locked his altimeter at night, and then crashed because he thought he was 1,000 ft up. Then there are

adjustable seats with insufficiently positive locking. Several accidents have occurred through the pilot departing rapidly out of reach of the controls during acceleration to take off. On the matter of seats one aeroplane had the fire extinguisher positioned under the pilot's seat (because no design provision for it had been made elsewhere). One day an extra large pilot was flying the aircraft, and feeling a bit cramped, pushed the seat back to the limit of its adjustment. This broke the seal on the extinguisher which promptly discharged itself. The pilot had to use his oxygen supply – which he was fortunate in having – to stop being suffocated before he could find somewhere to land.

In the original Boeing 707 the sensors for the compasses were placed in the centre-section of the aeroplane, a position giving least accelerations. On test the compasses read accurately, but as soon as the Boeing 707 first went into service the compasses went haywire. Everything was checked, and on re-test everything was in order. Back in service the same thing happened. Then it was realised that the hat-rack was on the inside of the cabin walling from the sensors, and along with the hats went transistor radios, and camera light meters, both ideal for confusing compasses.

Flying appears to suffer from an excess of ergonomic weaknesses because sophisticated and complex equipment offers plenty of opportunity for unintelligent design. It is also the most regulated of any of the activities under consideration. Unfortunately, because of the very fact of being airborne, and unable to stop or be rescued, the effect of any such weaknesses or failures is more critical, often unfunny, and invariably excessively costly. Of course aeroplanes do not by any means hold a monopoly in poor design. Plastic rowlocks break when the rower is having to pull really hard against an adverse tide, some motor cruiser cabin doors open inwards – the same way as the big waves go, non-slip decks do, cockpit drain holes are too small, and there is an almost infinite lack of standardisation in the operation of fire extinguishers, flares (though this is improving), direction of movement of engine controls, ignition switches, etc. Nevertheless in the area of the smaller, less expensive, and more widely used equipment, such as canoes, adjustable buoyancy life-jackets (A.B.L.J.s) for diving, caribiners and jumars for climbing, baskets for hot-air balloons, or echo-sounders for small cruising boats, there is a wide range of really excellent, high-standard, equipment available. It is in this sort of large and open market where customer pressure works at its best, and poorer quality material is as quickly as possible discarded for something that will do the job better.

Low-quality Ergonomics

Ergonomic weaknesses are mainly those in which the engineering is poor, and those in which an operator problem arises from poor presentation, lack of standardisation, or because the required manual movement is in an unnatural or illogical sense. It is not intended to go into the engineering aspects here, other than to say that some failures appear to stem from inadequate appreciation that the equipment *will* be operated by a fallible human who does not properly know how it works or what the dangers are, and under field conditions which may not only be severe, but quite different from those imagined by the designer. As simple examples, parachutists have threaded their chest harness straps through the ripcord handle, and motor glider designers have allowed too little clearance between the propeller tips and the ground, so that there are breakages when operating from the normally rough grass of some gliding fields. On one car of well-known make it is impossible to drive with the driver's ventilation slot open as the draught aims directly at the eyes, making them quickly sore. Presumably all the testing of this vehicle was done either by a driver wearing spectacles or sun-glasses, or with the ventilator shut.

Testing Programmes

One reason that weaknesses are not always discovered at the testing stage is that the tests, however rigorous, are usually done to a schedule, which although comprehensive, is in effect a programme; the tester is looking for what he expects to go wrong. He is also a skilled operator – otherwise he supposedly would not be doing the job – and as such he will tend to carry out the tests in a controlled manner. Subsequently the equipment fails unexpectedly, or is used incorrectly, and an accident results; because the operator used it in a way that had not been foreseen due to his limited skill and knowledge, because he was carrying too great an overload, or was frightened, or because he instinctively used it in the wrong sense 'because he was used to working it the other way'. In gliders, pilots used sometimes to pull the spoiler (airbrake) knob instead of the cable release, or do this and wonder why the spoilers did not open on the approach, until a worldwide convention was established that all glider cable-release knobs should be painted yellow. But on most cars with automatic transmission the order of the selector lever movement is still illogical. Park is forward, which is the natural movement for go, as in accelerators and aeroplane throttles. Reverse is also forward of Drive. Logically, and therefore easier to get right, the order from forward to aft (back) should have been Drive, D2, D1, Neutral, Reverse and Park with a gate. It should not be forgotten that any positive effort needed to become practised in the use of unnatural movement or sequence may contribute to subsequent misuse of logical order controls, the mind having been pre-programmed to control in the 'wrong sense'. In non-critical operations sequence and standardisation may not seem important – 'you can get used to anything'. It is in stress and overload situations that confusion occurs just when it is least needed; the inexperienced operator and his problems should be of constant concern in test programmes.

One area in which sound ergonomic understanding and extremely good design is necessary is where the memory is likely to fail, such as with undercarriage warning lights; where the equipment may be going wrong – low-on-oil warning lights; or where there is some other need, such as for anti-theft devices. If the design is not 100 per cent, so that the device is unreliable or easy prey to human errors, the end result may be worse than if the device did not exist at all. More than one pilot has broken an aeroplane making a precautionary landing on a false alarm caused by the failure of a microswitch. Sometimes, as with anti-theft car steering locks the 'safety' situation develops secondary complications. The lock was introduced so that the car could not be steered without the ignition key being inserted. But incidents have resulted from the car being moved, as when on tow, without the ignition key being switched to the first position, making it uncontrollable. Some cars require an additional action, using both hands, before the keys can be removed and the steering locked; a reasonable guarantee against taking the key out without thinking or even intent. No longer can a girl whip out the keys and throw them out of the window with the cry of 'No further will I drive with you.' Now the car could arrive in the cabbage field only seconds after the keys. Fortunately few people are as beset with warning signals as the airline pilot. In some jets the sheer quantity of warning signals can be almost an accident source in itself.

Performance as Described

Complaints are occasionally made that the performance of the boat, glider, or aeroplane is not as advertised, but the operational performance of a piece of equipment can rarely reach the optimum. The best performance of which the equipment is capable requires it to be used with great precision, which for various reasons, including shortage of skill or just not trying very hard, is not achieved. Loss of optimum performance may also be due to the gustiness of the air or wind, the choppiness of the water, or the condition of the equipment; a dusty glider or even a few barnacles on the boat bottom will work wonders in taking the edge off performance. When it is necessary to use equipment to the limit, as when clawing a sailing boat off a lee shore, or making a long, low approach to the airfield in a glider, optimum performance should not be expected.

11 ◇ PROTECT THE OPERATOR

In the event of failure to avoid the accident a disastrous end may be obviated or reduced by the use of protective items, such as crash helmets or life-jackets, or by the manner in which the equipment itself protects the operator; or at least does not add to any injuries. But safety cannot be just bought by writing out a cheque; many safety items have to be understood, and all used carefully if they are to do the job. Otherwise it is not difficult to make the situation even less safe. It is in this area that the designer needs a special and comprehensive knowledge of the operational problems – which means, especially, how they will be used and how they will work in adverse situations.

Survival Equipment

There are many solutions to the problem of how to stay afloat. The designer has to consider the sort and size of person who will be the user, how the device will be employed, and in what circumstance. He has to discover if there may be user aversion for any reason. Is it going to be too expensive for every purchaser? is it dependent on regular maintenance to retain its quality? and so on. Broadly, there are three levels of personal buoyancy. The first is the life-jacket, which is intended to keep a person afloat and the right way up for long periods with the head clear of the water, even if unconscious. They are expensive, but are sensible for any-one sailing off shore, or who cannot swim. Then there is the buoyancy aid, which is just what it says – an aid to keep a conscious person afloat while he rights his dinghy, or where the boat is operating close to the shore, or where there are plenty of other boats around, or when the water is warm. It is not so important that the person cannot actually swim if he does not mind being in the water. The third, the A.B.L.J., is a specialised flotation system for divers, which carries its own small air bottle, or can use air from the diver's main tank. When down the diver can adjust his neutral buoyancy by letting small amounts of air into or out of the jacket. Neoprene wet suits obtain much of their insulation from the minute nitrogen bubbles contained in the material. At depth these bubbles are squashed by water pressure and so the diver finds himself becoming heavier; and he counteracts this with a small squirt of air into his A.B.L.J. Actual figures are that an ordinary wet suit has about 8 kg buoyancy on the surface, half this at 10 m depth, and only 2 kg 30 m down.

On cruising boats an alternative to the life-jacket is a safety harness; instead of falling off and staying afloat, the sailor is prevented from departing the ship. The equivalent equipment to the life-jacket for the pilot is his parachute, and for the parachutist, his reserve parachute. All these items have certain things in common – they are useless unless they are either readily to hand when the drama unexpectedly begins, like life-jackets, or they are on and *properly* adjusted, as must be parachutes and A.B.L.J.s. The correct way to wear and/or use them must be obvious and straightforward, they must stand up to the work expected of them, and they must not add to the problem after they have ceased to be useful, e.g. it must be possible to discard a parachute quickly to avoid being dragged along the ground. Finally they have to be easily maintained by the owner, or servicing agencies must be available and efficient. Because life-jackets and parachutes are useful only in an emergency, it has to be accepted that the operator, at that precise moment, is very likely to be working inefficiently. He may be cold or injured, exhausted, frightened, confused, or all these things at once.

A 2-seater glider was on an advanced aerobatic training flight on a warm summer day. The student was in the front seat, wearing dark glasses against the glare, with the instructor in the rear cockpit. Near the end of the exercise, at about 1,700 ft, the student allowed too much slip to develop instead of executing the manoeuvre cleanly. This distorted the canopy and allowed the not very cleverly designed latch pin to disengage. The front half of the canopy flew off. Usually if a canopy departs in flight it blows clear over the tail, but this canopy hit the elevator and jammed it. The glider, now in a diving attitude at about 50–60 knots speed, offered no reasonable opportunity for the instructor to attempt to regain control, so he told the student to bale out. He then jettisoned the rear half of the canopy, so that as soon as he could see that the student had got clear he would be able to follow him without any delay. Their height was now 1,500 ft, but it was not until it was only 1,200 ft above the ground that the student actually clambered out and disappeared over the side. Relieved of his weight the glider reared nose-up, stalled and flicked over, with the instructor trying to get out on the port side. This was his only means of exit as the rear part of the canopy had embedded itself in the starboard wing, having only become partly free from the glider. The glider now rolled violently to starboard, pinning him to the port wing. With the ground now alarmingly close the instructor was beginning to run out of ideas when the roll continued until the glider was inverted, and he simply fell off. He looked up at the wing until he reckoned the parachute would not foul it, and then pulled the ripcord. The parachute opened and within 2–3 sec of it doing so the instructor went into the trees. The student landed on concrete but neither were hurt.

In no way could they have escaped if the parachutes had not been worn properly or the pilots not known exactly what to do. Even so, disaster was brought nearer than needed by that common affliction in any overload situation – fixation on irrelevant detail. The 300-ft delay in the student baling out, which could have cost the instructor his life, was due to the student deciding that he must not on any account lose his expensive new sunglasses. With great care he took them off and put them in a pocket before leaving the aircraft. Even on the way down, with the out-of-control glider and the temporarily trapped instructor whistling past not far away he was busy finding the case from another pocket, and putting his glasses in it so they would not get broken on landing.

If in circumstances like these something can be done wrong or some extra problem intrude it will do so.

Similarity is Confusion

During the war and for some years afterwards several pilots baling out of damaged aircraft were killed, because in the few seconds available to them they released the parachute harness in the cockpit in error, they then left the aircraft either without it at all, or with it only partly attached. The reason was simple. There was nothing wrong with the parachute harness release mechanism, except that it was virtually identical with the aircraft seat harness mechanism, and both were situated on the chest. In order to release either of these quickly, you gave the locking box a half twist and then banged it. The straps then fell out of the locking box. A pilot trying to bale out twisted and banged, but feeling himself still tight in the cockpit, did it again, and with great relief found himself free; not realising that on the first go he had banged open his parachute harness release box. Pilots were of

course warned against this possibility, even if the risk had not already become apparent, but in the moment of stress this particular problem was forgotten. It is still possible to fly with pairs of similar lock boxes, but today there is much less need to bale out in anger!

Life-jackets are usually straightforward, often with 'this way up' clearly printed on them, though buoyancy aids sometimes have attachment weaknesses such as lace-up fronts – which can be slow when you are all thumbs, or zips – even slower if you cannot start them. One small problem with buoyancy aids is that many are aimed at what might be called the holiday end of the market. To encourage people to wear them they are styled, or made of glamorous but less hard wearing materials, which does not necessarily add to their utility. Wet suits provide plenty of buoyancy, but wearing a life-jacket as well does not necessarily double the safety, as the flotation in the arms and legs of a full wet suit may be enough to prevent the life-jacket doing its job of turning the body right side up.

Straps, Harnesses and Seat-belts

Safety harnesses on boats, or glider and aeroplane harnesses, are, like car seat-belts, restraints intended to keep the user in the right place. They are least valuable when not worn or adjusted correctly. Boat safety harnesses may fail – fail to save the sailor, that is – because the caribiner or clips do not close fully through corrosion, because the rope was never strong enough, or is now chafed, or because the harness is worn too loosely. Most chest and twin shoulder-strap harnesses will not come off if too loose, but the chest clip may strike the user in the throat or mouth as he is brought up at the end of his line. Practically every glider in the world is fitted with full shoulder harness, as are many of the traditional British light aeroplanes. Over the years this habit has saved countless lives and heads and faces. Many American light aeroplanes still have only lap straps, although in the last few years there has been a move to change to full harnesses.

The wearing of harnesses, or for that matter life-jackets or crash helmets, is not only affected, but largely controlled by what people think others will think of them. Certainly a few individualists will wear some item of safety equipment in splendid isolation, but they are the minority. In general most people will do what most other people do. Even a car driver who normally wears a seat-belt may not do so when his passenger is a strong personality who 'never wears one'. This fear, or dislike, of being thought nervous, or a slave to convention, or merely a sheep is strong. A few glider pilots use their parachutes as a cushion, not doing up the straps; small-boat sailors, particularly anglers, tuck their life-jackets in the bow cuddy – about the most difficult place to retrieve them from in a swamping boat; car drivers have their seat-belts lying all over the floor; and some people are not even consistent. One extremely safe professional airline pilot, who was also an able and careful sailor, never did up his car seat-belt, and drove like a demon. Some divers leave their A.B.L.J.s in the dive boat, and do not display a 'Diver's Down' flag either, and a few hang glider pilots and white water canoeists do not wear helmets. Certainly, people can be made to wear helmets by law; as with motorcyclists, or parachutes or life-jackets by rules, but the only really successful way, in the long run, to encourage people to use safety equipment is because they want to. This means that they have thought about the problem and are prepared to take responsibility for their own necks. If in their considered opinion it is sensible to make use of aids to safety, they will do so regardless of what others may be doing. Attitudes of mind inculcated during training are an important factor here. If the sailing or flying school, or uncle or friend who provide instruction teach the proper use of safety equipment at the early stage, when the beginner is enthusiastically sopping up all the information going, the chances are that the habit will stick. If the instructor is sloppy and careless, or metaphorically allocates safety items to the nursery, then the student will do the same.

Deciding the Risks

It is very easy to say that life-jackets, crash helmets etc., should be worn whenever there might be any risk, but this can rapidly move into the ridiculous. In recreational sports, outside of competitions where there may be special rules, safety items should be used without question or argument when it is sensible to do so. And this goes back to the individual's sense of responsibility, and his ability to anticipate, or the extent to which he thinks about possible problems. The considerations, of course, should take account of others for whom responsibility is carried, and even of possible rescuers. One boat owner refused to carry flares on the grounds that his disasters were his own problem, and not anyone else's. But life is not like that. If the owner of that boat hit floating debris – not uncommon – a few miles off shore at night, and was sinking, a few red flares would bring a near-by vessel or a lifeboat to his aid quickly, cheaply, and without any unnecessary risk. But his non-arrival home could end up with an extensive search by boats, long-range aircraft, helicopters etc., over a wide area; and searches are not only expensive and time-consuming, but may have to be carried out in more hazardous weather than had earlier existed. Entire lifeboat and helicopter crews have been lost, when not even searching in the area where the accident originally occured. In a simpler situation, a dinghy helmsman without means of buoyancy would be less able to help an inexperienced crew.

Balancing the Risks

But if going to sea without flares, or without life-jackets is considered irresponsible or thoughtless, when is it sensible to utilise safety items and when not? Would it not be much easier to have a set of rules, or at least conventions, and stick to them?

This is one of the most difficult areas in which individual responsibility has to work, because it requires a balancing of the risks. To correctly assess risk it is necessary to have considerable experience, and experience takes time to acquire. To balance the risks it is necessary to expend quite a lot of thinking time. As an example, it is conventional in soaring gliding to wear a parachute. In years gone by this was because gliders were structurally weak and flew in thunderstorms. Now they are very strong, and rarely enter cu-nbs, but there are also many more gliders, and when thermal soaring they are flown in close proximity to each other. If they collide, and they occasionally do, the parachute exists as a means of escape. But for elementary training in 2-seater gliders, parachutes are not usually worn. The 2-seater may be soared in thermals with other gliders and is constantly flown in the higher density air traffic that exists around airfields. At first glance, it might seem even more necessary to wear a parachute during training than later when skill and experience is greater. The risk is there, certainly, but it has to be balanced with two very real considerations. Firstly, the student must know how to use the parachute. This takes time, and early on this instruction may do little to help build his confidence. Also, the student pilot flying for fun is doing so only part time and maybe with little money. Concentration in the first instance must be on teaching him how to fly *properly*. There is little sense in trying to teach him how to operate a parachute at a time when he is still probably insufficiently orientated in the air to get around to using it. Secondly, a parachute is no use unless it fits and is in good condition. With perhaps 3–4 different shaped students flying in each hour, the parachute would need to be frequently adjusted; further, with being constantly put in and out of the cockpit with the straps getting caught up in the controls, or left on the damp ground, the wear and tear on the parachute would soon exceed the capability – in terms of spares and maintenance charges – of keeping it serviceable. The balance therefore is between the possible saving of life should a collision occur in training at a height great enough to use the parachute, and the possibilities of the student having a badly adjusted or beat-up parachute, and also not using it properly. Experience, brought into this equation, indicates that a collision risk during training with an instructor on board is very small $2\frac{1}{2}$ million – 1 fatal collision in flights over a 10–year period. The time to introduce the wearing of parachutes in gliders is when the pupil is solo. He is feeling proud of his new skills and looks on his parachute as part of his improved status. With the basic flying behind him, he is better able to take in and understand instruction in the use and care of his parachute. There is also a good chance that he will look after it better than if it was a somewhat tatty legacy from his early training days. It is, of course, possible to be wrong in the balancing of risks, but nevertheless the effort has to be made, because in 'risk' activities it is an everyday problem.

In gliders there is no question that the wearing of crash helmets would reduce head injuries in the event of a crash, but this has to be balanced against the restricted peripheral vision caused not only by the helmet itself, but by limitations imposed on head movements in a small cockpit. When thermal soaring with perhaps twenty other gliders the risk of collision would be increased out of proportion to any reduction of head injuries in other crashes. Some pilots even turn peaked sun caps backwards when thermalling, so as to obtain maximum view and freedom of head movement. In military and commercial airline flying risk balances have to be made, but the considerations in making them are likely to be quite different from those in spare-time recreational activities.

When to Wear a Life-jacket

There are perhaps a million cruising boats sailing about and here the balancing of risks in terms of when to wear life-jackets or harnesses can be as complicated as juggling with half a dozen tumblers. The only fixed datum is that whatever the skipper decides is what has to happen. But the skipper – maybe with his first boat – still has to work out what the risks are and how they should be balanced. It is just as silly for an entire crew to sit sweating in life-jackets in warm sheltered harbour waters, as it is for a fore-deck crew to change a jib in a cold, choppy sea without one. The considerations are many, and include the security of the cockpit; amount of deckwork; the weather; temperature of the water; swimming ability; children being carried; type of passage being made.

Remembering that most life-jackets add to bodily warmth, restrict movement to some extent, and may be thought by the wearer to show him up as a beginner, or nervous, there is no sense in wearing a life-jacket when it is not necessary. Friends who can swim, for example, sitting in a deepish cruising boat cockpit and being taken for a coastal sail on a warm quiet summer day do not need life-jackets. They should know where they are kept, and how to put them on, but they should not be required to wear them. On the other hand non-swimmers or poor swimmers, who are frightened of being in the water, should be taken along only if they agree to wear life-jackets all the time when at sea. Children should have life-jackets, or if small preferably wear a safety harness attached to the boat, except when in the cabin. They should not be allowed to ride on the bows of motor cruisers unless their harness line will prevent them falling off if the boat suddenly stops. Small planing boats with powerful engines decelerate with remarkable abruptness when the engine fails. Anyone sitting on the bow will continue straight on, fall into the water, and be then run over by the boat and its propeller(s). The following wake wave may also catch up and swamp the boat. Conversely, if the throttle is opened suddenly the passengers not only may get left behind in the sea, but the boat may loop over on top of them. In order to avoid misuse some outboard designers provide a linkage which prevents the engine being started when in gear, and limits the throttle opening at this time.

With a competent crew working a sailing cruiser offshore, whether or not a life-jacket or harness is worn for deck work should be consideration of the chances of going overboard, the temperature of the water, and the skill of whoever is left aboard to find, reach, or avoid running over the person in the water. Crews familiar with their own boat, doing routine work like jib changing, on a moderately choppy summer day will probably do the job more quickly if they are not encumbered by either a life-jacket or harness, and will be perfectly safe. But if they are doing an unusual job like trying to retrieve a lost and flailing halyard, or the sea temperature is low, as it is in spring, or it is rough, or the helmsman is inexperienced, then common sense should dictate that additional security measures are sensible. In sailing dinghies – which are designed to capsize and float – life-jackets or at least buoyancy aids should be worn as a matter of course, unless the object is to explore shallow creeks on a summer evening or intentionally swim from the boat. The individual has to decide for himself what are the risks, and then act accordingly as a responsible person. Regulation is not the answer to the use of safety items where any balancing of risks is required. There was, and I think still is coastguard regulation in the States that required all boats to carry a recognised buoyancy aid for each person, which must not be secured to the boat. One dinghy load of adults, using their boat as a swimming and diving platform in secure and sheltered waters on a hot day, tied the life-jackets to a thwart to prevent them getting lost overboard while they were splashing about. They were fined.

Protect Them from Themselves

The case that is usually made for regulations is that people are not responsible and have to be protected from their own folly, quite apart from the protection of third parties. Superficially, it is sound reasoning since it is absolutely true that many people are at least careless and some are irresponsible. But regulations may not always reduce accidents in the long term – the only way is to dump responsibility firmly on to the individual, and give him practice in developing this rare gift before evolution loses it for him altogether. Balancing the risks will in some situations come down so heavily on the side of using some particular aid to safety that it becomes an accepted part of the scene. This may be because when it is needed it can't be fetched; like the sport parachutist reserve chute, but more because of the nature of the risk. In hang gliding the body is unprotected and even some minor error in flying technique may result in the ground being struck harder than intended. In older hang gliders with nose angles of around 90°, large in wing area, and slow, the flier used a seat harness, with his legs down, and with the control frame positioned almost centrally under the wing. The whole structure of the hang glider afforded him some protection because frequently something else hit the ground before he did. Newer, faster, hang gliders with a nose angle around 110° place the pilot nearer the nose and are usually also flown prone. The flier therefore is not only less well protected by the surrounding structure, but is leading with his head. There is no question that it is sensible to wear a good crash helmet. That this has been widely recognised is apparent in the development of special helmets with ear holes, so that the pilot can listen to air flow noise for the more accurate adjustment of his speed. Helmets with chin protector straps may look safer than those without, but with the strap worn on the chin the helmet is more likely to come off during the accident process. Police wear their helmets this way so that they can be quickly discarded. Parachutists and others who like to keep their helmet in place wear the strap well underneath the chin.

It is sensible to use aircraft restraint harnesses or car seat-belts when provided, as it will usually be impossible to put them on in time for the accident, particularly in a car. Certainly, it can be argued that there will be situations where the restraint can do more harm than good, fire being an often quoted example. But extensive research does show that the benefits of not using restraint systems are far outweighed by their correctly adjusted use.

Impact Speeds

The majority of accidents to gliders, light aeroplanes, cars and speedboats occur at speeds between 20 and 60 mph. Such crashes are, or can be, survivable; although last year no less than three speedboats driving into harbour walls were fatals.

The most obvious aid to survivability is that the cabin or framework containing people should hit the obstruction or the ground as slowly as possible. This is obviously not always controllable, but if, for example, a wing takes the first impact the cabin will follow less fast. The next need is for the occupants of the cabin to decelerate at the same rate. They cannot be made to decelerate more slowly, and are much more likely to decelerate at less than 50 per cent of the deceleration rate of the cabin through deformation of the seat, temporary deformation of the body, and because the restraint system was never adjusted tightly enough. During this deceleration process the occupants should as far as possible not strike instrument panels and such like, be injured by the restraint

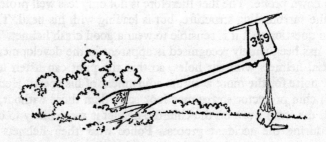

system itself (broken necks, stomach injuries) or have the restraint system – or the seat – come adrift.

It Matters What is Hit

In addition to the collapsability of the structure and the effectiveness or otherwise of the restraint system, the severity of the end result will also depend on the deformability of what is hit, such as muddy earth, concrete, or taking the wings off between two trees. Water can be very hard. It is often in the strength, shape, and freedom from projections in the surrounding structure that there is much room for improved design. In small aircraft the airframe and cockpit surround, as well as the instrument panel, are very close to the seats. With lap straps jackknifing of the top part of the body allows the head to hit any number of hard and sometimes sharp items at almost the same speed as the crash itself. But even with full harness the risk is still present, and is known. Nevertheless, the design of many small aircraft instrument panels present a sort of fakir's bed of knobs, switches, projection and even sharp edges, particularly at the bottom for the knees to strike.

The structural surround is usually equally lethal with sharp edges and unpadded pillars. Gliders are usually much better because the pilot is more supine in position and is well restrained by a 4, sometimes 5, strap harness. But whether or not the occupant decides to use any safety harness provided, statistics with cars – where there is a good, large sample to work from – show that in head-on accidents at around 30–40 mph the chances of becoming killed are almost exactly double when a seat-belt is not worn.

12 ◇ WILL IT STILL WORK?

For most people looking after some piece of equipment is a lot less enjoyable than using it. On boats or gliders maintenance takes a great deal of time, and can sometimes become very tedious. But good maintenance on such equipment is essential, and if it is not carried out it matters not how good everything was when new, nor even that the operator was highly skilled. If the boat rudder comes off because the hinge pintles corroded through, it may be wrecked against rocky cliffs however good the skipper. If a diver's air bottle blows up because the inside was rusted away, the well-painted exterior appearance is immaterial. Explosion is not the only problem with poorly maintained bottles, because rusting consumes oxygen, replacing it with ferrous hydroxide. The contents gauge gives no cause for alarm, but the proportion of oxygen in the 'air' may be down to 10 per cent or less instead of the usual 20–21 per cent. At 10 per cent it causes dizziness, 7 per cent stupor, and below 5 per cent it doesn't help you anymore. One diver went down to only 12 ft in a canal to recover an engine which had gone overboard. After 5 min his bubbles stopped coming up, because he had become unconscious and drowned, man being unable to detect lack of oxygen in the air he is breathing. Another diver died from the same cause but a different reason. He breathed directly from an airpocket in a rusty sunken barge, which was also too low on oxygen. Only good storage and maintenance and thorough periodic testing of bottles will keep them safe to use. It takes a quick-witted diver to diagnose that something is the matter with his air supply and get back to the surface before it is too late, just as it needs a very clever man indeed to quickly work out the causes, and then the cures, of some things that can happen in the air through poor maintenance.

Unexpected Aerodynamics

An Alaskan pilot flying a Cessna fitted with skis was on his way to collect some moose meat from a previous hunting trip. It was a fine clear winter day with an outside air temperature of 30° below zero. The first collection trip was uneventful, and in the afternoon he took off for a second load. As he was later than he intended he decided to fly a little faster than he had in the morning. On nearing his destination he reduced power and lowered the nose to maintain his speed. Suddenly with a violent lurch the aeroplane stood on its head, the pilot being flung upwards against the lap strap seat-belt, and his hand whisked from the stick. With the Cessna now screaming earthwards he managed to retrieve both the stick and throttle, closed the latter and started to try to pull gently out of the dive. Nothing happened. With the stick now hard back giving full-up elevator, the aeroplane was near its maximum permitted speed, and with the trees coming closer the pilot knew real terror. Instinctively, and without reason, there seemed only one thing left to do – push the stick forward. Remarkably, the aeroplane responded. Terror remained, because the aeroplane was now upside down, flying inverted and level, but below the surrounding tree-tops. Gingerly, he inched the nose up so the Cessna began to climb, remembering to use the controls in the opposite sense from when flying the right way up. As soon as he dared he rolled the Cessna upright, sinking close to the trees as he did so, and then climbed clear. Everything now seemed normal.

In a dream, almost unaware of anything except that he was still alive, he flew gently and slowly on to his destination and landed. After a few moments' reflection to regain his composure the pilot got out to look for damage and to try to discover what had gone wrong. Remarkably there was no damage. Then he realised that the reason for the aircraft's behaviour had been the skis. After take-off the toes of aeroplane skis are raised by rubber shock cords (bungees) so that they will not droop and dig in on landing. These shock cords on his aeroplane were a little too long, and the extreme cold had also reduced their elasticity, preventing the toes flipping up properly. When he had increased speed the airflow had instead flipped them both fully down, where they had acted as extremely powerful down-elevators. Only by continuing into inverted flight was he able to slow down sufficiently to regain control as the flapped skis now brought the nose up. An official publication on the rigging and maintenance of the skis and bungees existed, but neither had been properly followed.

No Propeller

Much nearer home a pilot was flying a small twin in November from Amsterdam to Southend when, in beautiful sunshine, half-way across the North Sea the left propeller just flew off. The pilot watched fascinated as it spun glittering into the blue sky hovering seemingly motionless. Then like a boomerang it arrived back on the engine it had left with a shattering crash. The cowlings split open, with oil and bits spraying in all directions. The opened cowlings became a powerful airbrake and at 150 knots the aeroplane slewed hard around in spite of full right rudder. With teeth-rattling vibration it was now all set to come apart. Quickly closing both throttles speed was reduced, which fortunately allowed the cowlings to return to a less high drag shape. At a slow 65 knots the pilot found it was possible to fly more or less straight, although sinking steadily down towards a fog bank with the North Sea under it. He contacted Southend on the radio as the twin subsided into the fog at 1,000 ft and still 10 miles from home. When just 250 ft up marshes appeared in the murk below. Visibility forward was almost non-existent so there was now the real added risk of flying into the power lines that criss-crossed this area.

Still flying with full right rudder, kept on by a foot trembling with a mixture of effort and fright, the aircraft vibrated on its way. Southend control kept giving bearings and distances, and control said that they would fire Very lights when the twin neared the runway threshold. At less than 100 ft on the rattling altimeter and with no further options open, the hoped-for Very light appeared ahead. Over the railway line, and with a last-minute decision to lower the undercarriage, the twin arrived on the ground, careering round in a huge ground loop before coming to rest. In the foggy silence all the pilot could hear was his own beating heart. The propeller nuts had never been properly locked.

Just Doing is Not Enough

One of the problems with essential maintenance – where it could be important to your continued existence – is ensuring not that it is 'done' but that it is done thoroughly. Otherwise a reliance

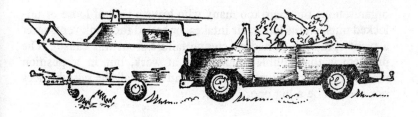

exists which is not justified; if something is known to be only doubtfully serviceable it can be treated and used with caution, and the operator is more mentally prepared for things to go wrong. It is easy, but not practicable, to say that anyone in a boat, glider, or whatever should be continually prepared for something to go wrong. Few people can sustain for any length of time the heightened awareness that goes along with emergencies. If they have done their homework and are operating sensibly within their experience, they should be able to enjoy what they are doing, and not need to live on the edge of a volcano. In general, maintenance of equipment is carried out either professionally or by the private operator. On all light aircraft, except those operated under the PFA (Popular Flying Association) the law requires maintenance and repair to be carried out by professional engineers. All the work on PFA aircraft and gliders can be done by the owner, but is subject to a schedule and inspection. Balloon pilots do their own maintenance to a set schedule. Hang gliders, all boats and mountaineering equipment are entirely under the control of the owner or operator. At the top end of the scale there will be no difference in the quality of the work carried out professionally or by the amateur. In a few cases the work of a really dedicated amateur will be better than that done professionally because of the unlimited time the latter is prepared to devote. At the bottom end the professional work will be of a far higher standard than that of the amateur – who sometimes does not get around to doing anything at all. At middle levels whether the work is carried out properly or not is dependent on how much the engineer or technician knows – usually appreciably more than the amateur – and how conscientiously he does his job. If he is not prepared to do this more thoroughly than a really good amateur, he should go and do something else.

Although there are many first-class servicing agencies and

organisations there are too many who leave a trail of loose or un-locked nuts, cloths left in air intakes, or sealed fuel tank vents after a paint spray job (I had an engine failure from this cause). The problem is that fallible humans are at work, but in a position where they are relied on not to err. And as usual, the mistake does not need to be a big one.

It Has to be Done Right

The pilot came to collect the Cherokee with his son on a poor December night. As an ex-wartime Spitfire pilot in current practice there was no lack of experience or skill. He checked over the aeroplane and ran it up. All the instruments read normally, and a very slight hot smell was put down to the de-mister operation which always produced a slight hot smell. The pilot and his son then took off for the Midlands. At 3,000 ft he monitored all instruments, and all were satisfactory. A few minutes later the engine revs started to increase rapidly, and he was only able to reduce them by partly closing the throttle, and loading the engine by keeping the aircraft in a slight climbing attitude – a situation inevitably leading to loss of speed or height. Putting out a PAN (in need of assistance) call the pilot tried to calculate which was the nearest airfield, and decided on Stanstead. The engine now started clattering, and the oil pressure dropped to zero. The compromise of retaining some power to try to reach Stanstead and not blowing up the engine was only partially satisfactory, and the aircraft lost height steadily.

The Cherokee was now in cloud, the night was pitch-black, and Stanstead was still 9 miles away. Suddenly the engine clattering increased, and before the pilot could shut it down completely it seized, leaving the propeller more upright than across, where it would have less change of damage. The pilot called Stanstead that his one and only engine had now stopped. He was at 2,500 ft with about 4 miles to run. Stanstead started to talk him down. The Cherokee glides with gear up at about 2 miles per 1,000 ft in nil wind; but it had a head wind. Flying at the best speed of 110 mph there was just $2\frac{1}{2}$ min of airborne time remaining. Still in cloud the instruments, no longer with the engine vacuum pump to drive them, were beginning to read doubtfully – a probability recognised by the pilot. He turned off the ignition switches, and the petrol – except that working only by feel he moved the cock instead to another tank. He switched off one radio and all electrics, so as to improve his night vision as quickly as possible. He checked that both seat harnesses were tight, using a tiny penlight he always carried when flying. At 700 ft the Cherokee came through the bottom of the cloud, and ahead were Stanstead's runway lights – but out of reach. The pilot's son unlocked and opened the door, so that it would not be deformed and jam when they hit the ground. The pilot asked Stanstead which part of the undershoot area was clearest of obstructions, and concentrated on flying straight, using the distant runway lights as a guide. But he saw nothing else until the aircraft ploughed into the ground. On this type of aircraft the undercarriage automatically lowers itself – in case the pilot has forgotten – when it is flown slowly at approach speed. In this situation this feature did more harm than good, ending with the wheels coming up through the wing; but had there been time for it to lock itself down, the aeroplane would probably have somersaulted violently, with even more dramatic results. As the Cherokee grated to a stop the pilot and his son leaped out and ran. When the aircraft was seen not to be catching fire the pilot returned and called Stanstead on the radio. The aircraft had luckily arrived into a soft muddy field. This however did not prevent looters and vandals arriving during the night, stealing £1,500 worth of radio and doing a further £1,000 worth of damage.

When the Cherokee had gone in for routine servicing the work was done correctly, but when it was being completed a mechanic replaced the oil drain plug with one intended for the same sort of Cherokee but with a fixed landing gear. He either did not know they were different, or did not appreciate that he was putting in the wrong one, although the fixed-gear plug shape has a projection which will foul the retractable nosewheel when it is raised. The projection was bent back and opened the oil drain.

It would be wrong to give the impression that professional workmanship is generally bad because of such an account of failure. The point being made is that if work is done by experts, a reliance is placed on this work, and the operator is expecting his equipment to be safer after servicing than it was before; not the other way round.

Maintenance is not Simple any more

Much of the sophisticated equipment in everyday use needs considerable technological understanding for its care and attention. Silicone cleaners, for example, used on a windscreen prevent it wetting properly, rendering the wipers less effective, and cleaners containing abrasives, however fine, are death to perspex canopies or screens. Emery papers used to clean commutators or contact points may subsequently cause shorting. Glass-fibre boats use polyester resin, and glass-fibre gliders use epoxy. There is also a practical need to know about electrolysis; it was enough for one aliminium boat to rub against a wooden jetty which was fastened with copper nails to later develop a complete row of holes in its hull.

Much amateur maintenance and repair is only average. This is sometimes due to lack of knowledge and skill in doing the necessary work – look at many patches on glass-fibre canoes – rough Isopon bodges (no reflection on Isopon), invariably light on resin, and with the canoe often used again before the polyester has fully cured, but more often it is as a result of those two human characteristics – procrastination and hope; the age of the average 'temporary repair' is probably about five years. A high standard of maintenance may not seem so necessary on boats, or skis etc., as it is on aircraft. One reason is that surface equipment can normally be made much stronger than it need be, because it does not have to be lifted into the air. Aircraft always have to be a compromise between strength and weight, and are designed to be only strong enough to do the job for which they are intended; and limitations, in terms of maximum speed, permitted aerobatics, and weight that can be carried, are placarded. It is usually cheaper to build something stronger than it need be if weight is no object, and with boats which may be caught out in near-storm conditions this is no disadvantage. The other reason why good maintenance may not seem so critical on boats is contained in the attitude that rescue is always a possibility; a disastrous policy on which to rely. Even though the largest call on the rescue services is due to broken-down motor boat engines, and even though most of these people are saved from their own folly, there are still some who are not. The catastrophically poor maintenance of some marine engines often originates from their very great reputation for reliability. 'Don't touch it, just put in the oil as the book says, and it won't give any trouble'; and perhaps for years it doesn't. Then it all happens at once – everything from failing ignition, to leaking stern glands, to corroded engine mountings, to fuel tanks with insides like a jumble sale. All that is needed is a rising wind and a rocky shore, or sometimes not even that.

Too Little, Too Late

A crew was bringing an otherwise well-equipped 42-ft motor cruiser powered by two 270-hp engines home across the Bay of Biscay in order to carry out a major overhaul after four years abroad, yet the voyage itself was one which demanded a really serviceable boat. After leaving Tenerife on course, it was noticed that the boat seemed to be somewhat too close to Gran Canary than had been intended – about 10° off the intended line. Landfall in the afternoon produced confusion in locating the anchorage in Lazarote, due to the boat being some 35 miles from its intended position. The next day they ran to Casablanca with no problems, but the 420 miles in a choppy sea took 31 hrs and left the crew weary.

The next leg was to Lisbon, departing Casablanca at 18.00. About midnight there was a crash as if something had been hit, but no water seemed to be coming aboard – other than the considerable wave spray from the rough sea. Then one of the windscreen wipers packed up due to a worn sprocket. Around 01.00, in the middle of refuelling the main tank from three of the seven 50-gallon drums on board, all the navigation lights fused – with other ships on possible collision courses. They were avoided, dawn broke with a confused sea but no further problems, and they continued on. Near Lisbon, in quieter weather they opened the forward hatch which it had not been safe to do earlier. About 4 ft of planking had been stove in from whatever they had hit in the dark, but the cascover sheathing over the hole had remarkably not given way. At Lisbon the damage was repaired with a glass-fibre patch. From here on was mostly bad weather and heavy rain; with the Bay of Biscay embarked upon with winds force 3–4, although not from a good direction. At about 100 miles out, at the point of no return, a new forecast was picked up giving force 5–6 NE. Bucking into the head wind and sea it was necessary to slow down to 8 knots instead of the usual 17. Then water was discovered to be pouring in through the aft cockpit bulkhead. Inspection showed 2 ft of water swirling about in the tiller flat.

Working the big bilge pump aided by a bucket reduced the quantity, but did nothing to prevent the continued inflow. However, it made it possible to see that a weld had failed in the stainless steel exhaust pipe, which was now leaking engine cooling water into the boat. This was not too serious and could have been contained, but wrapping a towel around the leak caused the entire weld to collapse, giving a 15-cm entry to the sea. With everyone needed to pump and bale to keep afloat meant that not even the most temporary of repairs could be started; and the water was gaining. The realisation that they now had at most 5 min before sinking came as quite a shock. To send out a mayday call, prepare the inflatable dinghy, grab emergency supplies, and put on life-jackets meant that pumping had to be stopped. Even collecting the emergency supplies produced a problem as there was no plastic container of drinking water and the main supply was now under water. All that could be found was a bottle of brandy. No reply was received from the mayday call. The set was working but with VHF not good for much more than 30 miles on the surface, the Bay of Biscay seemed a big place. As the water rose up to the stern gunwales, two got in the dinghy but the Spanish crewman then would not do so; refusing to believe that the dinghy was safer than the big cruiser; but he was finally enticed in. Then they watched their boat, all lights blazing, disappear. There were few ships around the horizon, and the waves were 12 ft high, so it was not unexpected that the first pyrotechnic display of flares produced no instant aid. They conserved the remainder for a while and attended to various small leaks in the inflatable. Just before dawn they sent up a parachute flare which produced no response from a ship a mile or so downwind. The Spanish crewman stood up and shouted, and nearly fell in – or out. Five hours later with only two flares left they saw a cargo ship on a converging course. They were just about to fire the flares when on the other side a large liner was seen coming straight for them. Now there were other problems. Dead in line with the rising sun, the flares would be all but invisible, and the liner could drive straight over them without even knowing it. They fired the first flare and waved a yellow oilskin. The liner thundered on, passing close enough to throw the dinghy around in its wash. They fired the last flare with a hopeless feeling. The liner watch officer did not see the flare, but noticed the residual trail of dirty smoke that it left. It was the Norwegian cruise ship *Oslofjord* that picked them up.

Faith is Not Enough

Perhaps the most common example of faith in so-called maintenance occurs with small two-stroke outboard engines. They exist in their thousands and so cannot be considered as rare items that no one knows anything about. It is only necessary to use a two-stroke for a day, or even talk to an owner to discover that although well made and basically reliable, they can also be temperamental. They do not always like running slowly and will oil up plugs when most inconvenient; and they suck seaweed into the cooling water intake and seize up. Usually much sooner than later outboards have to be worked on while the boat is bouncing about on the sea. All that is usually required is a new, correct specification plug and a plug spanner in a plastic bag, yet hope springs so eternally that even these small items are not often carried. Often second-order repair items such as oars, paddles, or sails are not carried either. Even well-found cruising yachts can sometimes be seen powering along, with mainsail covers on, and with no jib ready, in restricted waters where engine, fuel, or cooling failure could rapidly become highly embarrassing.

It Happens Too, When New

One does not normally associate maintenance problems with new equipment, but if the quality control and final servicing has not been done properly, the problem can be just as serious as a failure to maintain. Since it seems a fact of life that much new equipment seems to need to be 'run in' before it is right, it is sensible not only to give it the best inspection of which the new owner is capable, but to use it initially in easy and safe conditions.

User unfamiliarity may additionally add to any problems. With boats, balloons, or gliders, it is often easier said than done to 'send it back to the makers' after the damage has been done. A new 35-ft yacht, for example, is expensive, but one delivered to its proud purchaser lasted less than a day. He was aiming to reach his destination along the coast at 21.00 hrs on a May evening, when about 6 miles short the diesel stopped through apparent lack of fuel. Sail was hoisted and the boat proceeded on its way. Within distant sight of the harbour entrance the snap shackles holding the jib sheets to the jib failed and the yacht made considerable leeway whilst the repair was done. It was now dark, but surprisingly no lights could be seen. The echo-sounder was working only intermittently, thought to be on account of flat batteries. At 00.30 the boat went aground on a falling tide shortly after a reading of 12 fathoms (72 ft) had been obtained on the echo-sounder. Sails were taken down, the dinghy was put over the side to lay out a kedge anchor to seaward. The main anchor was put out and distress flares fired. It was then discovered that there was a layer of lifted fog at 20 or 30 ft above the surface. No one saw the flares. By now the yacht was on its side, dry, and without damage. The lifeboat arrived soon afterwards, having been alerted by a friend expecting the arrival of the boat. The crew were taken off in the dark, then the weather changed and before any attempt to save the boat could be made the wind had increased so much that it was battered to pieces by 7-ft waves.

Beaten by a Bird

Using any equipment in a substandard condition is a potent and frequent factor in accidents, but is not often enough realised as such, particularly when the risk to life does not appear to be great, as when a sailing dinghy rudder breaks or comes adrift sailing on a small lake or reservoir. But care of equipment is an integral part of any activity, and should be looked on this way. Apart from defeating the twin demons of procrastination and hope, good maintenance requires determination and persistence – to ensure that some trouble has been properly cured. Occasionally this determination may even be two-way, as when a pilot lost power on take-off, returned, landed, and on a more thorough inspection discovered a birds' nest in the carburettor air-intake. It seemed a mystery as to how the birds had got in behind the wire gauze

screens, but they had. The only other possible way in was by one of the two emergency air-intakes which were covered with spring-loaded flaps. In some way the birds had discovered that these flaps gave entry, and had then learned to let themselves out again by prizing open the flap door with their beaks. The nest was removed. A few days later the pilot returned and peered into the intake, and there was a brand-new nest.

13 ◇ PROPELLERS ARE HARD

However well things like boats and aeroplanes are designed, there is likely to be some item or feature which is thoroughly dangerous, and which is not amenable to having this characteristic designed out of it. Propellers are the most obvious and they are very dangerous. Accidents are only avoidable by understanding the problem and by working to strict, self-imposed rules, drills or procedures. The same applies with other equipment in use such as free-running anchor chains, which can bite a leg off at the same time as tossing its owner into the sea, winches which are excellent for jamming fingers, or climbing-ropes which will burn into hands.

Flying Without a Pilot

There are two quite distinct sorts of accident which can happen with propellers whether they are on a boat or an aeroplane. They can kill or injure, and they create quite remarkable runaway dramas. The most interesting that I have actually seen was the aeroplane towing a glider without a pilot in either. It was all quite simple, really. The tug aeroplane was to tow the new glider to a purchaser across the Channel from a customs airfield. Without the

facilities of a gliding club the two pilots positioned the two aircraft, and attached the tow rope to the nose of the glider and the tail of the tug. The glider pilot got in, closed the canopy and waited. The tug pilot went to swing the propeller, but the engine did not start. So he walked around the wing to the cockpit, switched off the ignition, opened the throttle, and returned to the propeller to blow out the too-rich mixture. He then went back to the cockpit, and in his impatience to get going switched on the ignition but forgot to close the throttle. In this act he was not unique; before the days of the electric starters it happened all the time. He returned to the nose and swung the prop. The engine fired and the aeroplane at once started to accelerate. Dodging out of the way the pilot grabbed at the wing to try to hold it, but was shrugged off and knocked down for his trouble.

The glider pilot realised at once that he must *do* something, but in the heat of the moment merely achieved a hopeless but heroic act. Instead of just releasing the cable and staying safe, he jumped out to try to hold the glider back and thus slow down the aeroplane.

This forlorn gesture merely resulted in his being knocked down as well; while the tug and glider waltzed away over the grass airfield. Without the pilot's weight in the nose the glider climbed steeply, stalled gently, climbed again, then stalled sharply and dived into the ground. The aeroplane got airborne only to take the next hedge in a fine failed-Grand-National style.

Some years earlier a slow, lightly loaded Klemm aeroplane took off empty for exactly the same reason. It flew around over Kent and Sussex hotly, but unsuccessfully and dangerously, pursued by people in cars. Eventually, its fuel exhausted, it glided down and landed without damage in a large field.

Recently the same thing happened *again*, but this time there was a fifty-year-old non-pilot woman passenger inside the aircraft. It climbed away to 5,000 ft. The woman without knowledge, or even help from the radio, as she did not know how to switch it on, tried to teach herself to fly. After some 15–20 min she attempted a landing, but caught a wing on the ground, somersaulted along the runway and was killed.

Driving a ski-boat alone a woman turned so sharply to pick up a fallen skier, that she centrifuged herself out of the boat. On full lock the boat ran round in circles and twice ran over its driver. Remarkably she remained alive.

Walking into Props

If runaway accidents are foolish and expensive they are fortunately not so often lethal, unlike the accidents where people walk into the propellers of aircraft stationary on the ground. About twenty people a year in the United States alone walk into props – for every reason; adults, children, passengers, ground crew, even pilots. About 25 per cent of these people are killed, the others severely injured. During the Second World War a Wellington on a training flight made a bad landing at dusk. The instructor got out to inspect the undercarriage leaving the engines running. He looked at the leg assembly from the back, examined it from the side, looked closely at it from the front, and then walked backwards to check its alignment. It was only when he saw the propeller rotating in front of him that he realised that he had walked backwards straight through the slowly rotating prop.

The reason most people walk into props is not usually that they do not know that it is dangerous, but have a moment of aberration, forgetfulness, or concentration on something else. Since even pilots and engineers who have worked on aeroplanes for years walk into props the only way to be sure that the next time it will not be you, or your friends, is to never allow *anyone* to get into or out of an aeroplane with the propeller turning, unless they are being personally escorted by a sensible person and the escorted route is safe, as when the entry door is behind the wing. All other times the engine *must be switched off*, no matter whether it is temperamental and difficult to re-start or not. Swinging a prop should never be attempted unless there is someone in the cockpit who understands what he is doing, the brakes are on, and if the surface is hard and smooth or slippery, chocks are used in front of the wheels as well. It should be checked that the person in the cockpit knows what is meant by 'contact' and 'switches off', and *repeats* the order. If he has never propped an aircraft before, he must be given a dry run and it must be checked that his shoes will not slip, and that he is not wearing any clothing that could be caught in the prop. It may seem all very dictatorial to go on about what is after all a very simple matter, but it is an easy and messy way to get hurt.

Because nothing in this world is perfect, ignition switches may not work properly, and even when they do it is still possible for a hot engine to fire the prop around at least once; and there are also different types of switches. One flying school had just finished re-equipping itself with new aircraft which used an ignition-key system like a car instead of a tumbler switch, as previously. A student pilot showing this glamorous fleet in the hangar to his friend pulled over a prop having thought the key was positioned to 'off'. Being a fine new aeroplane it started at once and roared around the hangar, not stopping until it had eaten five of its fellows with its own now chewed-up prop. Helicopter rotors can of course be walked into as well, but one pilot in a lightweight helicopter jumped out to pick up a package leaving the rotor running. Relieved of his weight the helicopter rose sedately into the air and then fell expensively on its side.

Stop the Prop – but how?

Occasionally dramas produced by propellers have other primary causes. A small Dutch coaster caught fire and put out a mayday. The intensity of the blaze prevented the crew from getting near the main engine controls to stop it. So off drove the coaster straight for the Isle of Man like an outsize Olympic torch, with the crew and the captain's wife clear of the smoke on the foredeck. Several naval and other ships, including HMS *Bronington*, set off in pursuit. Then the coaster suddenly changed direction, probably because the automatic pilot incinerated itself. A helicopter attempted to winch the crew off the foredeck before the boat blew up, but the near-gale that was blowing, plus the coaster's speed made this impossible. A naval ship then fired a line to try to transfer the crew, but this did not work either, so the *Bronington* put her Gemini inflatable in the water, and this managed to get alongside and take off four people. Having transferred them to the mother ship it went back to try again. The coaster was now hell-bent for Strangford Lough where the alerted locals were launching lifeboats and anything else that seemed useful. Just before hitting the shore the coaster's engine finally burnt up as well, and the propeller finally stopped. The skipper let go both anchors, and the fiery stern grounded on the shore. *Bronington*'s Gemini, still hanging on like a terrier, took off the remaining crew, and everyone breathed again. But not for long; on a later high tide the coaster refloated *and* reignited itself before finally sinking.

Stop the Prop – like Now!

The accidents that most frequently happen with small boat propellers occur when the boat is moving, and is being used to pick up swimmers or capsized dinghy crews. On a boat the propeller really is invisible, and if the skipper needs to keep the engine running to succeed in a pick-up, he may have a real problem. If the swimmers, or divers, are in the water for fun propellers should be stopped and the boat anchored or allowed to drift. If there are any reasons at all why the engine should be kept running, and the prop cannot be stopped, then it is no place to swim. The emergency or 'in difficulties' situation may be different, as when people in the water are being picked up in a restricted tideway. The skipper has to appreciate that people in need of rescue seldom act rationally, and may have to be kept forcibly from grabbing the boat in the region of the propeller, and he has to carry this responsibility, whether he likes or not.

PART THREE

♢ *Special Problems*

14 ✧ TEMPERATURE, PRESSURE
AND SUNDRY POISONS

In addition to the great variety of errors made all the time, like forgetting things or being complacent, the human body itself contributes further interesting shortcomings. It is particularly good at this as soon as it moves out of the limited environment to which it has adapted itself for so long. It does not like being too cold or too hot, and becomes thoroughly temperamental when the pressure or the quantity or quality of the air it likes to breathe is altered.

Cold

Cold makes perhaps the most common contribution to accidents because it is so easy to get cold, particularly at sea, and cold reduces the efficiency of the operator by making him lethargic, clumsy and slow-witted. The human body cools twenty-seven times faster in water than in air, but people vary considerably in their reaction to cold. One seventy-year-old Swede fell through ice when crossing a lake and was in the water nearly half an hour. When he was pulled out his body-temperature was 28 °C instead of the normal 37 °C. Most people would have died, though it is thought that he survived because of the rapidity with which he was cooled. Hypothermia is a well-known problem and much advice is given as to how it should be dealt with. But perhaps the most likely person to be faced with coping with a hypothermic victim is the small-boat sailor who picks someone out of the water. On board his facilities are severely limited, as is his speed to land, and maybe also his ability to summon suitable aid. So what should he do? Probably the best thing is to take off the victim's outer garments and any others that are holding a lot of water, and put him as quickly as possible into the best situation of maximum insulation from the evaporative outside air and keep him quiet and secure. Trying to strip him of all wet clothes in a small and possibly gyrating cabin may be slow and disturbing and the victim may lose remaining body warmth. This, in the average small boat cabin will probably mean putting him inside two or three sleeping bags plus adding any woolly hats, pillows, plastic covers, sails, or anything else that will help in the impermeability of his surface surroundings – and then hope.

Air and its Goodness

Pressure and the quality of the air are the special concern of both the flier and the diver, and in certain respects their problems are similar. On the surface of the earth the air pressure stays around 1013.2 mb, rarely subsiding below 960 mb in the centre of a deep depression or rising much above 1040 mb in the centre of an anticyclone; extremes that are well within ordinary human tolerance. Most people do not even notice the change, although a few complain of rheumaticky pains when the pressure is low or of headaches when it is high. But as soon as altitude is gained, by flying or climbing a mountain, the lowering pressure and the changing quality of the air begin to be noticed. Skiers above 8,000 ft probably feel some breathlessness, and glider pilots above 12,000–15,000 ft will fly less competently, although they may not realise this at the time.

As the pressure lowers the air becomes 'thinner' although its constitution of approximately 21 per cent oxygen, 78 per cent nitrogen and 1 per cent carbon dioxide and other gases remains the same. It might seem that by just breathing faster the body will obtain all the oxygen needed, but it does not work out like this. Even at sea-level the amount of oxygen taken in with each breath is less than 21 per cent of the whole because of added water vapour. With every breath of good air taken in the lungs are at the same time trying to off-load a quantity of carbon dioxide, produced in exchange for the oxygen; so there is quite a lot of this around too. At sea-level the resultant reduced proportion, or partial pressure, of oxygen is satisfactory, but it becomes increasingly less so with height. The pressure of the water vapour and carbon dioxide in the lungs remains relatively constant, but the fall in the oxygen and nitrogen intake pressure steadily increases. The lungs become

starved not of air, but of oxygen. All that a speed-up in breathing rate would do is to increase even further the proportion of carbon dioxide in the lungs.

High Flying

The effect of shortage of oxygen, hypoxia, varies with health and age. Some people begin to feel the effect as low as 12,000–14,000 ft, but by 20,000 ft few remain conscious, let alone sensible. Symptoms include dizziness, tiredness, headache, blurred vision, blue finger-nails, constant yawning, and most dangerous of all, a feeling of well-being. If flying is contemplated above 10,000 ft oxygen should be carried. Above 12,000 ft it should be used whether any symptoms have appeared or not, particularly if the pilot is working hard at decision making, as a glider pilot would be. By 15,000 ft it should certainly be used.

Abel Sintora, an Argentine glider pilot was soaring locally in a Blanik glider for some cloud flying practice, on a day on which thunderstorms were developing. He climbed in one cloud to 15,000 ft, then left it because he had no oxygen. He flew off into a strong downdraught and was soon down to 7,000 ft, so decided to return to the airfield and land. His route back took him through the bottom of a cloud, and in it he suddenly felt himself hit a violent upcurrent, with the variometer showing 6,500 ft per minute climb. Despite his efforts to fly out of cloud on a compass heading, and when this was unsuccessful by putting the glider into a spin, the Blanik went relentlessly on up. Sintora vaguely noticed the altimeter reading 22,000 ft and ice on the wings and canopy. Then he passed out.

He regained consciousness to find himself quite low in a left-hand diving turn, and then passed out once more. When he awoke again he was lying in the crashed remains of the Blanik, which had hit sloping ground at a flat angle. Discovering himself to be alive and to have sustained only a cut on his face and a damaged ankle, Sintora, in wonderment, started to look about him. The first thing he noticed was that his Blanik was missing about 12 ft of each wing, including the ailerons. Then he looked at his baragraph; the almost vertical trace went up to 41,600 ft at which height the recording needle became jammed at the top of the drum. An airline pilot later provided the information that the cu-nb in which Sintora must have been sucked up had topped out at 50,000 ft. The wings probably broke somewhere near this height. As well as having the incredible luck to stay alive, Sintora ended up with the Argentine height record as well. Apart from surviving the actual crash, he almost certainly survived such serious oxygen starvation because of the rapidity with which he was sucked up and subsequently fell to earth. In fact, the glider coming apart was the unexpected saving factor!

Going Down

If the human sets off downwards below the earth's surface, in air, as when pot-holing, there is no real problem either in the quality of the air that he breathes, or from increased pressure. Even down a 1,000-ft mine, the air pressure will be only some 30 mb higher than on the surface, well within tolerance. In water it is all different. Below the surface it is the effect of pressure rather than the quality of the air which causes the greater difficulty, because the compressed air supply, in use all the time, regulates itself to supply air at whatever pressure (depth) the supply finds itself. For all normal diving the breathing mixture is ordinary standard air, although usually drier than that outside. Pure oxygen is unsatisfactory for breathing below about 30 ft, because when compressed it poisons the diver. It is only at depths of 150 ft plus that ordinary compressed air becomes unsatisfactory, and a breathing mixture containing helium instead of nitrogen is better – apart from the squeaky effect it has on the voice, normally known as the Donald Duck sound.

The Bends

The big problem of rapidly increasing pressure with the depth of water is that gases become dissolved in the bloodstream; when pressure reduces again, as the diver ascends, the gases come out of solution. Oxygen and carbon dioxide do this rapidly, but nitrogen does not. It transfers only slowly. If the diver goes deep enough or stays down long enough for the nitrogen to become dispersed around the body in his bloodstream, it will effervesce into bubbles if he comes up too quickly. This is the bends, which can be painful, paralysing, or fatal. The cure is recompression in a chamber under medical supervision. If no decompression sickness is apparent, but it is known that the diver ascended more quickly than permitted by the tables, he should return to a depth of 20–30 ft with a further air supply for long enough to give the nitrogen bubbles time to disperse.

Flying and Diving

Diving combined with flying increases the chances of getting the bends. Every diver should possess the published decompression tables which show how long a diver can stay at any depth without having decompression problems; very roughly this is about maximum 60 ft for maximum 60 min. If the diver stays shallower the tables will tell him how much longer he can stay down, and also how much he is restricted in time if he goes deeper. But these tables are calculated on the normal surface air pressure of 15 psi. If the diver now takes to the air up to say, 8,000 ft – the usual jet cabin pressure – the effect on the nitrogen bubble problem is as though he had been diving deeper than he actually had. So he may find he is developing an attack of the bends soaring in his glider, or eating his plastic lunch in an airliner. The

simplest rule when combining diving and flying in any 24–36 hr period is to limit the dive to a maximum depth of 50 ft. Tables for flying after diving are given in the RN Manual and RNPL tables.

Nitrogen Narcosis

The other problem with nitrogen is that it becomes toxic with increasing depth, which is why it is replaced with inert helium. Nitrogen narcosis produces symptoms not dissimilar from those of inebriation. In addition to the effect that the increased pressure at greater depth has on the body itself, the deeper diver has to cope with a change in his buoyancy. This is mainly caused by compression of the tiny nitrogen bubbles in his wet suit, which makes both the suit and the diver increasingly less buoyant as he descends. At about 100 ft down he may well be negatively buoyant. This compression of the wet suit also reduces its insulating properties, so that he will more rapidly become colder. The experienced diver will understand these problems, and because he does will probably not suffer from the real psychological effects of being so far from his natural element, and being unable or forbidden to get back there quickly.

Underwater and Underbuoyant

The waters in the Caribbean are clear and delightful for diving, and there is plenty of opportunity to indulge. A man and wife, both newly certificated and tested elementary divers, joined a group for some pleasurable holiday activity. Their deepest dive so far had been 25 ft, but unlike some they had no real ambition to head on down. On the last day of the holiday the dive leader decided to organise a deep dive to 200 ft. The couple, quite rightly believing this to be beyond them, decided to go along with the group, but break off at 100 ft and slowly return to the surface together.

The group went into the clear, warm water and swam over the edge of the reef down to some 50 ft. The coral was fascinating to look at, their equipment was working with no trouble, and it was all very relaxing. At 100 ft the man turned to signal to his wife that the time had come to surface, but she was not looking. He attracted the attention of the dive leader to signal her to go up, and cleared with him that they were now departing. By this time they were down to 125 ft. As they started up the husband checked that his wife was a little above him, swimming vertically upwards, as he was. He then checked his depth gauge and was shocked to find it reading 135 ft; so spent a little time wondering if it had gone wrong. The face of the reef was still visible only about 20 ft away, and below was still complete blackness. It frightened him to look down. He looked up for his wife, but she was no longer there. In such isolation a feeling of panic began to creep over him, and he tried to fight it off by checking on his still plentiful air supply and on his depth gauge – except that showed him slipping ever deeper; he was swimming up and yet going down. When the depth gauge read 150 ft the feeling of panic became so irresistible that he wanted to tear off his mask and tank and somehow just escape, because he knew he would die if he could not get free. He noticed he had been breathing slowly, and started breathing rapidly, because, since he was dying anyway, there was no sense in not using up the air. The fast breathing noise was loud and worsened the panic. Terror was just about to overwhelm him absolutely, when he suddenly saw another diver staring at him through his face mask. Shaking with fear he motioned him over and more than anything wanted to touch this link with life, but knew that if he did so he would grab uncontrollably. Surprisingly, the other diver did not seem to be showing concern, and this had a calming effect. The other diver signalled OK?, and because he did not know what else to do, he returned the signal; discovering at the same time that a few hard kicks helped him to ascend. The other diver stayed with him until they reached about 60 ft, then left to rejoin his own group. He surfaced, and swam over to the dive boat, feeling calm, until he found that his wife was not there. The other group then appeared and she was not with them either. He was convinced now that she must be dead. Then a boat arrived towing her along, alive. She had reached 175 ft just as unintentionally, but she had then let some air into her A.B.L.J. Suddenly, he remembered that in his panic he had completely forgotten his own life-jacket, and that at any time he had had the means of arresting his terrifying descent; but he had been so confused by fear and disorientation, and bemused by the increasingly toxic effect of the nitrogen that he had been incapable of doing anything sensible at all.

C_O Poisoning

One breathing problem that the diver does not suffer from, unless the compressor used to fill his tanks has taken in polluted air, is carbon monoxide poisoning. This gas is produced by incomplete combustion of fuels and lubricants. It is colourless, odourless and tasteless, and it combines with haemoglobin, the oxygen-carrying agent in the blood. Because its affinity for haemoglobin is greater than that of oxygen, this becomes excluded, and the blood is starved. The symptoms are feelings of sluggishness, feeling too warm, and headache, followed by dizziness, and eyesight dimming. Unless the good fresh air can be obtained at this stage loss of muscular power and unconsciousness follow. Carbon monoxide poisoning is particularly insidious because the gas gives no hint of its presence. Up in the air its effect can become severe very rapidly, because of the reduced proportion of oxygen that exists anyway.

In light aeroplanes which normally fly with all windows closed, a cracked exhaust may not take long to permit the amount of carbon monoxide in the cabin air to reach a serious level; and it is made even worse by smoking. One woman had the shattering experience of having to sail a boat home on her own with her husband dead in the cabin. Coming off watch, he went below for a rest, and a faulty engine exhaust system did the rest.

Disorientation

Another serious shortcoming of the human body is the ease with which it can become completely disorientated unless its feet are planted firmly on the ground. In certain circumstances even this is not true, if the eyes are confused by optical illusions; look at a 360° movie screen when you are standing up, and you can be made to feel you are leaning over.

Disorientation is a state of confusion concerning a person's true position in relation to the normal surface of the earth. It is caused primarily by the eyes being deprived of visual references, like the horizon, but also by misleading information supplied by the inner ear balance mechanism, and failure of the special muscle sense, proprioception, to inform the brain what is happening to the body; 'flying by the seat of your pants' is a proprioception benefit.

Although when diving one can become so disorientated that it is only possible to tell which is up by looking at what is happening to the discarded air bubbles, and then heading off that way, disorientation is a more common problem when flying in cloud. Without instruments and the ability to interpret them the pilot, deprived of any visual reference, soon ceases to fly straight. The aircraft starts to turn and its speed varies. This adds the even more confusing effects of acceleration, so that the pilot is soon without any reliable information about what is happening. Now his inner ear balance mechanism muddles him further, because of its lag tendency. If the pilot manages to retain control and come out of the turn and fly straight while still in cloud, his balance mechanism will tell him that he is now turning the other way and he will suffer from vertigo.

Disorientation need not be a hazard, provided it is appreciated how it can occur, and what it feels like. It is something most pilots are aware of, although some do not manage to avoid weather situations in which they become disorientated with disastrous results. It is not so often realised, however, that a car driver, speeding along a motorway and running suddenly into fog, also suffers disorientation. His judgement of speed and direction, which are normally monitored constantly by visual reference, is now unexpectedly without this means of control. When a car or a tree suddenly appears the driver is unable to judge his relation to it in time to attempt to avoid it.

Negative g

If the aircraft is accelerating in a positive g sense, as when pulling out of a dive, the pilot will be compressed down into his seat. If the g is negative, he will be propelled up against his straps, leaving his seat, even if only momentarily. These forces can disorientate an inexperienced pilot even in clear air, particularly if the pilot, not understanding what is happening, confuses negative g with being stalled. A number of gliding accidents have occurred following the cable breaking on a winch launch, when in order to regain speed from the nose-high attitude on the launch the pilot pushed the stick sharply forward to avoid stalling. The immediate feeling of weightlessness convinced him that he had now stalled, and in desperation he pushed the stick even farther forward to regain speed. Too late he realised that he was about to hit the ground in a dive. Student glider pilots now are given a mild demonstration of negative g sensation in a two-seater to help them recognise it.

Drink and Drugs

Drink and drugs are an increasing source of accidents not only because many people's consumption has increased in recent years, but because some medications are quite sophisticated in the way they work – unlike the old-time purge – and because drink and drugs may react undesirably on each other. Whereas most people have, or think they have, a pretty good idea of how they are affected by alcohol, the same cannot be said of drugs. Worse, there seems to be a coyness among some doctors to provide essential information on side-effects. If the activity to be carried out is likely to be at all demanding – and any flight, or dive, or mountain climb, or solo boat operation is demanding – then it is essential that skill and judgement are not impaired: no one is always all that good even at their brightest. Anti-hystamines, sea-sick pills and tranquillisers may be especially effective at producing drowsiness, inattention, depression, impaired depth perception and dizziness. Amphetamines can diminish natural feelings of fatigue, produce euphoria, and tend to push the body beyond its natural capacity. They are all contributions to calamity which can be done without.

Few people fly or set off on some enterprise knowing themselves to be inebriated. More do so without realising that they may have had too much to drink. Attitudes to alcohol change with time and place, and so do people's consumption capabilities. What is important is that each person should develop a responsible attitude to his own drinking, decide on his limits, and not go beyond them. There are people who will not touch alcohol if they are going to fly within 8 hrs, and others who consider that a beer or a glass of wine with a meal however shortly before flying does not count as drinking. There is no doubt that the effect of alcohol varies in its effect on a person, depending on his health, tiredness, and what he is doing. Quantities of cold or fresh air and exercise, as with skiing or sailing, seem to quickly evaporate away any alcoholic effect from, say, a pint of beer, whereas the same quantity consumed in a small, warm, smoke-filled cabin may produce quite a different effect. If people are to recognise that they may have drunk more than intended, then the symptoms need to be known. One is dimming of the eyesight, like wearing dark glasses at twilight, but perhaps the main one, and more difficult to recognise, is the deterioration of judgement. The reason why this disability is masked is that reasonably small amounts of alcohol can actually improve a person's handling of a car or aeroplane. The brain ceases to be cluttered by doubts, and the aircraft will be landed beautifully on a short runway, or the car driven fast into the garage without touching a thing. All very pleasing, except that no judgement has been involved. The short runway was not the runway in use, but luckily no other aeroplane happened to be coming in at the time, and the car driver could not possibly have stopped had something been left in the middle of the garage floor. Hangovers, being more tediously apparent than the primary effects of liquor, are often persuaded to vanish by consumption of coffee. But as one doctor said about imbibing caffeine on top of alcohol, 'It does nothing except produce a wideawake drunk.'

Judgement Departs

A helicopter arrived on a barrier reef island around noon, and was not scheduled to leave until the following day. For lunch, during the afternoon, and before, during and after dinner the pilot had some drinks quietly with his wife and friends, enjoying a restful day. Shortly before midnight a flare was seen out to sea, and a faint discharge sound heard. Two hotel guests told the manager of the distress flares, and he and the local boatman went down to the beach. After reckoning they could see a flickering white light on the horizon, they rowed out in the boat to a couple of small ocean-going vessels to ask for help. No reply came from the first ship and no help from the second. Neither owned up to say that the flares had, in fact, been fired from one of the two boats. The helicopter pilot was just going to bed when one of the hotel staff told him about the flares, so he, too, went to the beach. After looking for a few minutes at the white light he said he was sure there was someone out there and that something had to be done. He added that although reluctant he would if necessary use the helicopter to assist the people in trouble. The manager and boatman then put an outboard on the dinghy and set off again, together with the pilot, hoping to see something shown up by the frequent lightning flashes from a near-by thunderstorm. But the boat could not get across the coral reef and returned after a half-hour sortie. Back on the beach the manager was not keen on continuing the search, but the pilot seemed convinced that there was a boat in distress, and after some further discussion, went to prepare the helicopter. He had some 6,500 hrs flying and about 400 hrs of night and instrument time, although he had not done any night flying recently. The manager and the boatman went to the helicopter, and the three took off. The lights of the helicopter were seen to pass low over the trees and out to sea, to move round in a gentle turn low down, and then disappear. A sound of impact was heard. Several small boats now went out, but initially nothing could be found. At about two-thirty in the morning a small light on the water was noticed, which turned out to be the emergency light on the helicopter's self-inflating dinghy. This was still attached to the wreckage of the helicopter which was on the bottom in shallow water. Although the pilot should never have embarked on this enterprise, he did so with the best intentions. His judgement was impaired by alcohol, and further affected by thoughts of two fishermen from the island who had recently lost their lives, and it was said that had a helicopter been around at the time they could have been saved. When all other means of resolving whether or not on this particular night there was a boat in distress, the pilot had taken upon himself the burden of further action. It is not unusual for someone affected by alcohol to form a strong opinion based on insufficient evidence, and in this case, although reluctant to use the helicopter at night, and knowing he had been drinking, the pilot eventually decided to go.

15 ◇ COLLISION

As if all the confusions that the operator is able to create for himself were not enough, collisions have to be added to the list; those exciting or infuriating moments when someone else and his property clashes with you and yours.

Collisions are unnecessary, but the plentiful causes include:

Neither seeing the other;

Neither looking out because the chance of collision is remote;

One sees the other and assumes he has also been seen;

One sees the other and, being in the right, assumes the other will avoid him;

One or other, or both, are ignorant of the rules.

It is not so usual for a collision to occur with neither party seeing the other at all. It does occasionally happen, as when a submarine, some years ago, undoubtedly assuming it was entering Dartmouth, bounded up the shelving beach at Slapton sands and sent a cyclist flying. Much more common is for one party to see the other and make assumptions that do not turn out to be the case, as did the pilot of a floatplane who was about to land on a river where he had a camp. There was almost no wind, and near touch-down the pilot saw a powerboat about to cross his path from the left. He thought the boat would be clear of him and so continued on, but then saw it turn and head for his landing position. Instead of opening up and going round again he shifted his touch-down position to the left, assuming that the boat driver would now see him and turn away. He did not, so the pilot diverged from his landing line some more, hit a rock on landing and overturned. There is only one safe assumption to be made, and that is that the other party is not looking, and act accordingly. This does not mean that everyone should weave around in permanent avoiding actions. There are rules of the road, sea, and air, and these should be followed until it becomes obvious that other measures are likely to be needed. The operator should be mentally prepared to have to take the initiative, and not just sit there until it all happens.

Two is Enough

Perhaps the greatest risk of collision is when it is assumed that there is no risk. When fifteen or twenty gliders are circling together in one small thermal it might be fair to think that the risk of collision is greater than when there are only two or three. This is not so. The risk in the crowded thermal is small for the simple reason that the danger is apparent; so everyone in the thermal keeps their eyes peeled. With only a few gliders there is plenty of room for everyone, not such a good look-out is kept, and the actual risk is higher. At a club in Austria only two gliders were evening flying, doing circuits of a few minutes' duration launched alternately by one winch. It would be difficult to organise a collision in these circumstances, yet the two gliders hit each other head-on while coming in to land.

Eyes are for Looking

A formation collision with a difference occurred when a Rapide and an Islander were lifting a fourteen-man parachute team to 12,000 ft for a jump. When they were ready to go the two aeroplanes were throttled back, flying quite close to each other. The six parachutists from the Rapide and four from the Islander departed but as they did so the two aeroplanes started to close in on each other with the Rapide losing height. Number five from the Islander came out and was horrified to find himself hurtling past the Rapide with only inches to spare. Out came number six. He hit the top of the Rapide fuselage breaking his leg, then rolled clear and opened his parachute. By now number seven was on his way. He went straight through the top of the Rapide fuselage and finished up on the passenger cabin floor with two broken wrists. Number eight just managed to stop himself in time. No one expected the other aeroplane to be there, where it definitely should not have been, so no one saw any reason to look.

Rules are for Knowing

In waters where the density of boats racing, tacking, fishing or capsizing is high there are very few collisions. The realisation

comes quickly that as well as keeping a good look-out it is necessary to know the rules, even if these merely allow one helmsman
to claim priority over another. Skill is developed in avoiding not
only a collision, but collision situations. But it does not, of course,
need two moving objects to create a collision. One expensive
yacht was sailed straight into a heavyweight navigational buoy,
opened up like a tulip, and sank. This could have been because
no one was looking out, or because of the Mesmerisation Effect.
I first learnt of this very many years ago when watching a friend
teach himself to ski on a slope some 3 km long and 1 km wide.
The only break in the otherwise blemishless surface was a baby
fir tree about a metre high. Incredibly, it seemed at the time, one
of his skis went each side.

Making Eyes Work

Eyesight is obviously a major factor in collision avoidance, and
the first thing to recognise is that there is a difference between
ability to see and seeing. The most perfect eyesight is under-
employed if it does not know what it is looking for or how to
recognise it. Some people with only average eyesight will unerringly
spot buoys among the waves or distant aircraft in the sky, because
they have learnt how to make the best use of their eyes. Eyes
suffer from a number of limitations as well as absence of direction
from the brain. Although they can see things through the very
wide angle of 200°, they only actually focus and concentrate on
objects within an angle of 10–15°. And it is only objects within
this narrow range about which the brain is informed. The old
phrase of 'seeing something out of the corner of your eye' really
means that you thought you saw something but are not quite sure.
The limitation of the unfocused peripheral vision is overcome by
scanning; using the eyes to track slowly back and forth across the
area of sea or sky that is important to study.

The next problem is that even within the 10–15° angle the eye
will not focus properly if it does not have anything to focus on.
One reason that a pilot may not see that distant aircraft even if
his eyes are pointing towards it, is that they are not focused at
the right range, or not focused at all. This goes by the name of
'empty field myopia'. It is overcome by halting the scan at intervals

and deliberately focusing the eyes as though trying to study objects at different distances. Once this habit is formed it is easy to do; and is only what those people who are good at spotting things do without thinking.

When flying it is always hoped that any other aircraft that could be a threat has been seen, but sometimes only the shadow of an aircraft on the ground is visible. If the shadow is of the pilot's own aircraft it will have a bright spot on it, and the pilot can relax. If it does not it is a possible adversary.

Eyes have Problems, Too

Having learnt to look and to see, the eyes may still let their owner down because they are readily affected by dust, salt, dazzle, glare, age, fatigue, emotion, hypoxia, hangovers, optical illusions and dark glasses. It takes about 10 sec for the eyes to sort out information – to see, identify and persuade the brain to initiate action – and a lot can happen in 10 sec.

Leaving out the more mundane things that afflict the eyesight, like age and hangovers, by contrast optical illusions and dark glasses deserve special mention. An optical illusion is quite simply that what you are seeing is not what it actually is. A real problem exists when flying at night if the pilot stares for a long time at a fixed light. After a while it appears to be moving irregularly from side to side. If he has no other visual references he endeavours to keep the light still by controlling the aeroplane appropriately. This gets him nowhere quite fast. The same happens, of course, on a boat on a calm night, but the effect of chasing the light to 'keep it fixed' is not so fraught. This little difficulty is known as stare vision. Even in daylight a pilot approaching a strange airfield which is situated on an upslope can get himself in trouble. Being used to going into 'flat' airfields he expects to see the runways in the usual perspective. But the runways on the upslope look to him like a flat airfield when he is coming into land with too much height. So he lets himself get lower until the airfield looks like he expects it to look. Plenty of aircraft have hit obstructions on the approach path for this reason. The business of seeing what is expected to be seen is not confined to pilots. Most people from time to time see only what they are looking for, ranging from picking out the 'criminal' on an identity parade to the real illusion of the sailor long at sea, who sees land when none is there. Ship-wrecked and afloat in a liferaft he will conjure ship after ship from an empty horizon. The converse also happens, as when people become selectively blind to road or speed limit signs, particularly in their own locality. One aeroplane pilot arranged to formate on a helicopter to take photographs and flew into the arc of its rotor, because he did not see the blades although he knew they were there.

Drift and Relative Movement

Many collisions, in which both parties have seen the other, take place because of a failure to appreciate drift; the movement of a person or vehicle in a direction other than that in which they are pointing. In the air an aircraft normally flies along 'following its nose', and in addition, the wind may be drifting it sideways over the ground. Two aircraft in the air will be affected by drift equally. If they collide it will not be because one drifted into the other but because one or both pilots misjudged the closing speed. An aircraft coming into land can, of course, drift into a fixed object on the ground because only the airborne object is subject to drift.

On water the drift situation is more complicated, because boats are only half in one medium, the water, which may be carrying them in one direction; the other top half of the boats is in a different medium, the windy air. This may be trying to move them in another direction and the effect of the wind, or windage, of boats will also vary; a big container ship will be more subject to wind drift than will a small dinghy. The movement of boats relative to each other is not, therefore, always obvious, and an inexperienced sailor may not realise that a collision situation is developing until it is almost too late to do anything about it. It is, of course, for reasons of drift that big ships should be abandoned on the weather, or windy, side. The lee side may look calmer and safer, but the drift of the boat will quickly take it over any small objects, like persons or liferafts without even a pause in its progress.

Fixed objects, like navigational buoys in tideways, are very easy to collide with. With the water moving invisibly at 3 or 4 knots it is not in the least difficult to discover suddenly that the safe

distance originally allowed for passing it has somehow rapidly diminished, due to failure to appreciate the relative movement of the two objects.

One catamaran helmsman lost in windless fog in the channel decided to temporarily tie up to a navigational buoy as being the best way of avoiding being run down by some ship. Mooring line in hand he jumped on to the buoy to tie up. The sea was quite calm and smooth but the invisible tide was strong. Before he could secure his line the catamaran pulled it steadily through his fingers and silently drifted away into the fog, complete with his non-sailing wife. Fourteen hours later, when daylight returned and the mist dispersed, he was rescued from his perch by a passing boat.

Don't Obstruct the View

Good causes of collisions are what the operator has, or puts, between his eyes and where he is going; like dinghies stowed on cabin tops, deck-sweeping genoa sails, dirty diving-facemasks, inadequate aeroplane windows, maps or charts jammed into where there ought to be a view, thick spectacle rims, and dark glasses. Some gliding clubs do not use high-wing aeroplanes as tugs, because in a turn it is too difficult for the pilot to see what he is turning into. Gliders have good visibility canopies, because it is essential to be able to study the sky in order to stay airborne, and because they fly closely together in thermals. Dark glasses, good ones, are useful against glare and the almost dazzling conditions that occur in bright summer haze or with snow. They are not quite so useful on boats because much of the glare on water comes from below, and most glasses do not give protection in this direction. Glasses which adjust themselves to the intensity of light should be removed when the light or glare lessens, as they re-adapt themselves to weakening light more slowly than the eyes themselves. Even the eyes are not all that quick at dark adaptation, needing between 5 and 40 min depending on the person, hangovers, and other factors, and red is the best colour of artificial light to use if dark adaptation is not to be quickly lost.

Left and Right

Even when the adversary has been seen and action to avoid being struck decided, there is still another little human quirk which may come into the equation. It might not be putting it too strongly to say that about a third of the adult population do not know left from right, particularly in a sudden emergency. Shouting at the helmsman, or pilot, or canoe partner to go left may produce inter-esting results. If it is vital to go with great rapidity in the correct direction and it is possible to touch the person on the appropriate arm, this should be done.

Wildlife Collisions

Most collisions are between people or inanimate objects like buoys, television masts, or rocks, but wildlife should not be for-gotten. There seems to be two special risks – bird strikes for the flier, and whales for the ocean sailor. Bird strikes occur quite often, but, unlike most whales with boats, may not always do significant damage. Occasionally, however, the problem caused is unexpected. One aeroplane collided with a flock of gulls 50 ft up after take-off. The control tower was told of the incident and that the pilot intended landing back as soon as he could because the ailerons had jammed almost solid. With great care the pilot flat-turned around the circuit; then at 500 ft one engine lost power, and soon after stopped. The pilot managed to land successfully and inspection showed the fuel having gone from the port tanks – due to a seagull beak having opened the drain cock.

Man, His Own Enemy

But man is still his own worst enemy, proving that after all only one human is needed to make a collision. One US pilot tried to fly a small light plane from his strip on a day with several inches of snow, but failed to accelerate properly because of the slush and because his little runway was humpbacked in the middle. He even found it impossible to taxi back to his hangar, so he locked up the aeroplane, left it near the end of the strip, and went back to his business. After several hardworking days, he decided to fly his other aeroplane to a meeting. The snow had gone, and a pleasant breeze was blowing in a direction that would enable him to take off in his four-seater from the near, hangar end. Away he went, without a care in the world – until he charged over the hump straight into his own light plane.

As well as the more obvious causes of collision, there is often lack of appreciation that the people in the other boat, car, or air-craft could be having a problem. It is easy to assume that the only reason for the impending collision is the stupidity, or bloody-mindedness of the other party. But the other pilot may be lost and scared, or be trying to retrieve a failing engine, the helmsman of the boat may be exhausted with a seasick crew, and not feeling too well himself. A few years ago this radio conversation was recorded between an airport controller and the captain of a large aeroplane. It followed radio contact between the controller and the pilot of an Apache light plane which had lost all its navigation and cockpit lights through mechanical failure, and wanted urgently to land.

Control: Six Two. Turn left 320 now. The Apache doesn't have any lights.

Captain: We are flying visual, we do not need any vectors.
Control: OK. Do you have the Apache in sight? He has no lights on.
Captain: Well, you tell the Apache to get out of the way. We got our lights on.

16 ◇ CONFLAGRATION, EXPLOSION AND LOOSE ELECTRICITY

Some years ago I was flying a glider on aerotow in a formation of three over the Jugoslavian countryside, towed by three PO2 biplanes. The tow home would take a little over the hour, and we were flying very close together, because the Jugoslav pilots enjoyed flying in tight formation, and their aeroplanes were smaller than the gliders. Shortly after take-off the middle glider, piloted by a Swiss, started to fly in a most erratic manner. This was unexpected because we knew him to be a most competent pilot. We, on either side of him, watched this performance warily, ready to release if the collision risk became too high. He continued all the way home flying like someone inebriated. Arriving overhead our home airfield, the Swiss pilot released the tow rope, opened his air-brakes, and went rapidly down, while we released and stayed up in the evening sunshine as long as we could.

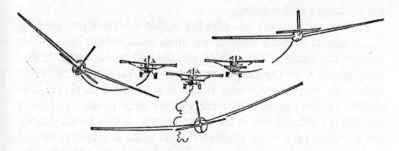

What had happened was that shortly after take-off the Swiss pilot had decided to have a smoke (permitted in fuelless gliders), but his box of non-safety matches had burst into flames and not surprisingly he had dropped them. The ball of fire disappeared out of reach under his plywood seat where the control cables lay.

Thoroughly alarmed in his wooden glider the pilot wondered whether to release and land in the unsafe-looking country below, jump out by parachute before this also caught alight, or hopefully try somehow to extinguish the fire. He kept feeling the base of the control column to see if it was getting warm, and wriggling about in his seat to distribute any hot spots his parachute might be acquiring. During one of these body shifts both bottom seat-harness straps came free, charred right through. None of this improved his formation flying capability. Becoming desperate now, he suddenly remembered that he had a bag of plums in his pocket. Laboriously he wrung out the meagre juice from each plum above where he hoped its dribbles would do most good. Not any too soon did the welcoming home airfield appear, and the Swiss pilot lost no time at all in getting back to earth. But for the last minutes of the flight there had, in fact, been no problem, because the fire had burnt through the bottom of the fuselage and fallen out. The Jugoslavs thought it was hilarious.

Last year a pilot stepping into a recently refuelled aeroplane, felt his foot skid across the metal floor on a crushed box of non-safety matches; and another pilot with two books of matches in his pocket had them flare when they shook against each other in turbulence. Another pilot smelt burning, which is very frightening anyway, and especially so if the aeroplane is too high to get down really quickly. The panel cigarette lighter had been pushed in by the passenger and jammed.

Perhaps the greatest risk with fire is that no one is prepared for it. Usually it happens without warning, unexpectedly, and it can be very frightening. The sudden sinking feeling of inevitable disaster mixed with the desperate urgency to 'do something' often ends with everyone running round like headless chickens. Undoubtedly, the original discoverers of fire were equally surprised. But fire is a definite risk in the air and at sea. It may be very small, but it exists. Like so many other things, when it occurs is not the time to start to learn what to do. Test pilots are used to the unexpected so it was not surprising that when a marquee caught fire at a big air display that they were the first people to react effectively, with soda siphons seized from the bar. In the past, most fires were simple combustions, mostly of wood, and could be extinguished by copious supplies of water. Now it is all much more complicated.

Electrical, petrol, or other chemical fires need different treatment, and do not always like being squirted with the wrong antidote. Some fires, and some extinguishers, produce toxic fumes. If this were not enough different extinguishers not only operate in different ways, but can become old, or corroded and not work at all. If a fire, almost any fire, is tackled quickly and correctly there is a very good chance that it can be controlled, and any damage limited. But this will only happen if at least one person on the spot has thought seriously about how to deal with fires, knows which extinguisher to use, how to operate it, and knows that it will work.

One person, who clearly had never appreciated that fires occurred outside fireplaces or on the ends of cigarettes, crashlanded in Canadian rough country after the aeroplane engine failed. Neither he nor his friend were hurt and after considering alternative plans for some time it was agreed that the passenger, experienced in the wilds, should walk out for help, while the pilot made himself as comfortable as he could for the night in an aeroplane sitting on its nose in a bog. The next morning the pilot, cold, hungry, but otherwise fit and well was delighted to hear the distant sound of a helicopter. Seizing the hand flares he jumped out, and when the helicopter was not too far away to see him against the low sun, he lighted one and waved it vigorously above his head. The helicopter turned and came his way. Overcome with excitement, as only the about-to-be rescued are, he jumped up and down and threw away the flare into the bog. Unfortunately, the leaking fuel tank had been feeding the bog all night. The conflagration was considerable by the time it had consumed both the aeroplane and a bit of Canada.

Most fires on boats, and in some houses, originate from the explosive gases from butane or propane cylinders used for cooking, or from a petrol/air mixture which has acquired the right proportion, between about 11-17:1. Natural gas needs twice the concentration of 'town' gas before exploding, but when it does it makes four times the bang. Only a short time ago a motorbike with fuel in the tank was taken inside a house so that the owner could do some work on it. In the confined space the mixture got itself just right. A match being struck resulted in serious damage to the whole house. One supposedly intelligent man did not realise that some gas cylinders have left-hand thread, and examined a slack connection on his calor gas container by match light, causing flame to start playing round the neck of the cylinder. This had a very remarkable effect on his grey cells. Instead of turning off the gas ring and quickly smothering the cylinder with a blanket, he ran several hundred yards down the road to the public telephone to ring up the calor gas agency at seven o'clock in the evening – to ask them what to do. By the time he had got no reply and returned, two pieces of the exploding cylinder had gone through the side of the caravan narrowly missing his wife, whom he had not told 'not wanting to worry her', and a large chunk had arrived in our garden 200 yds away.

Several boats each year blow up or are burnt in British waters alone, usually through the heavier-than-air gas sinking into the bilges and waiting for an opportunity. Care, scrupulous maintenance of piping and taps, installation and use of gas snifters all help, but do not provide any absolute guarantee against fire on board. The only absolute safeguard is that there shall be either no loose gas, *or* no flame or spark of any sort at all. There is no compromise.

During an exhilarating morning sail in his steel 5-tonner a single-handed sailor discovered, when he went below to brew up for lunch, that petrol had been spurting out around the filler cap and that there was probably now about a gallon in the bilges. As the fumes were strong he decided to drink water instead of tea. By about five in the afternoon the call for tea was strong but resisted, as in spite of ventilating the boat, the smell was still there. At 19.00 it became foggy and the engine was started – by cranking, not electric starting which is good value for initiating this sort of fire. At midnight a plug oiled up, and having no form of safe illumination the sailor decided to change the whole lot, rather than try in the dark to trace which one was causing the trouble. By feel the new plugs were screwed in and the high-tension leads attached. It was a quiet night and without other shipping about the job was done peacefully. He then swung the starting handle. In a great whoosh of flame he found himself on deck on his hands and knees, peering horrified through the hatch to what was already an inferno. The front of the echo-sounder melted and dripped before his astonished gaze. Then flames burst upwards through the hatch. All thumbs and trembling with the shock of it, the sailor hauled alongside the little pram dinghy that he had been towing and fell heavily into it. Immediately it filled and sank. He scrambled back on board, hauled the pram up by its painter to empty it, got into it more carefully, and sat looking at his boat. The metal sides were already glowing red, and the sea hissed around her. Then the flames subsided and night was made darker by the black smoke that now poured out of the hull. The sailor went back on board, aft where it was not too hot, and tried to see through the smoke, but the saloon was still glowing. He closed the hatch, hoping belatedly to smother the fire. He feverishly started throwing buckets of water down the companion way to try to save what was left of his beloved ship. Then he saw that she was sitting lower in the water, and realised that he was actually helping to sink her; so he stopped. By now he was gasping for breath, he had cut his hand, the boat was almost awash, and there was no other shipping in sight. After dithering about helplessly for a bit he returned to the dinghy, and watched in miserable disbelief as his boat sank, disappearing with a sound of rushing air, and leaving just a few bubbles on the surface. He sat for some time just looking at the empty sea, then suddenly feeling himself cold, he started rowing towards the flash of a light vessel some 5 miles away. He did not remember much of this journey, only the kindness shown him after being helped aboard.

Sparks and Static

Gas explosions of a different kind happen with balloons. Not the hot-air variety, which in spite of being powered by a naked flame equivalent in energy to about three domestic central-heating systems, very rarely burn themselves up. It is hydrogen-filled balloons that have the problem. They have been around longer than most other varieties of aviation, and although tragedies like the Hindenburg airship are well known, the risk is not great provided that there is no smoking, and no sparks from other sources. Herein lies the difficulty; a little matter of static electricity. Static can build up to an appreciable extent on electrically non-conductive surfaces such as plastics, including glass-fibre and nylon. Such surfaces generate more static when clean and dry, and less, perhaps none at all, when they are dirty or wet. Dry, clean nylon ropes or synthetic fabric clothing generate considerable static, like taking off a nylon sweater in the dark with its display of sparks and flashes. Clearly if such a source of sparks exists near a hydrogen balloon, the chance of a good blast-off becomes a probability. Natural fibres also generate static if they are very dry, but this is rarely the case with worn garments even on a dry day due to moisture replenishment from the body. Because of the static problems hydrogen balloons cannot reasonably take advantage of the wide range of synthetic fabrics that are available, as can hot-air balloons. But simple static is not the only problem with hydrogen balloons. If, or when, the gas they contain becomes diluted with air a burning, or an explosive, mixture will be created. Usually one leads to the other. Friction in the envelope, for example, while it is being collapsed, or if the hydrogen is allowed to exit too rapidly, may cause a spark and start a fire. This may not be immediately noticed because hydrogen flames are invisible. The fire, by changing the shape of the envelope, or burning a hole in it, allows more air to intrude, and bang she goes.

The famous balloon, Jambo, which had crossed part of Africa photographing wild game, was lost by fire and explosion. She was being emptied when a sudden gust of wind shook the balloon causing considerable friction in the neck and in the folds of the fabric. A small burn started followed by an explosion, which blew the top off the balloon. Sometimes water is sprayed on a hydrogen balloon during deflation to reduce the risks. Helium is safe, but expensive. Most balloonists now bypass this problem by using hot air. Aeroplanes are quite capable of generating enough static to get burnt or blown up during refuelling, unless the hose is earthed by using the clip for bonding it to the aircraft. Trouble is more likely if the aircraft is being fuelled from cans via a plastic funnel, as friction on this may produce a spark. Dangling loads from helicopters also become charged, and should be discharged other than via the unloader's body.

Too Many Volts

Most people only get fussed about static electricity when they receive a sharp tingle on the fingers from their own car doors. It

is not regarded in the same way as real electricity – lightning and the stuff supplied via the national grid, which is an efficient source of accidents and kills many people in their own homes every year. It is, also, perhaps surprisingly effective in killing small-boat owners on land. In the last 2–3 years about half a dozen sailing dinghy people have been electrocuted, apart from numerous but less disastrous incidents, by hitting power wires with the mast of a boat while moving it on its trolley. In nearly all cases it happened at an established sailing club, usually during an open meeting. The locals had no problem because they *knew* that their own class boat-masts had room to spare under the wires. The visitors, some with taller masts, just pushed their boats about like everyone else. Each time this accident happened it was given publicity in the American or British sailing press. To no avail; it happened again recently.

But it is always easy to be wise. When I was very young the railway near our home was electrified. There was much talk of this new development in our area and of how sheep were straying on to the live rail and being killed, because they were in contact with the line and the ground. Birds were safe because they could hop on to the live rail and no part of them touched the ground. After school we went along to try. It was true; if you jumped on the rail with both feet together and then cleanly off again, you did not get a shock. I still get goose pimples whenever I think of that day.

Power Wires

Light aeroplanes and gliders fly into power wires from time to time, most usually because they are not seen when low flying or approaching to land at an unfamiliar private strip, or when a glider is going in to a field landing. The problem with flying into power wires is not so much what happens to the pilot, since it was probably his fault, but the hazards to would-be rescuers if the lines are broken but the power still remains on.

A most calamitous example of this occurred not to a pilot, but to a motorist. In the early morning dark and rain the car skidded off the road, jumped a ditch and hit a pylon carrying a 15,000-volt supply. A live cable-end fell on the car roof with a shower of sparks and stayed there. Terrified of touching anything the driver sat absolutely still on the plastic seat, with her feet on the rubber floor mat. About 10 min later a truck stopped on the road and the driver ran across to help her. In spite of her screams for him to stay away, the driver grabbed the door handle and was instantly killed, his body falling in some bushes. Although it was still dark, another truck driver spotted the car and came to assist. Again the driver screamed and yelled for him to stay away, but the same thing happened. By the time a third truck came along and stopped it was light enough for him to see what had happened, and he drove away at high speed to get the electricity switched off. Not so many people in the same unhappy predicament would know that the driver could, in fact, have touched anything in the car, including opening the window and even getting out, provided that she did not touch the ground at the same time as the car. This is easier to say than to do. Apart from not necessarily having enough knowledge, there was the risk of displacing the power cable end, or inadvertently touching even the thin twigs of a bush.

Two men leaped off a yacht just before it hit a power wire. One went into the water and was unharmed. The other jumped cleanly on to the jetty, but in doing so a loose end of his jacket just touched the mast rigging and he was electrocuted.

Blitzkrieg

When it comes to natural electricity, lightning, the risks are limited to when there are thunderstorms in the vicinity, except occasionally for hydrogen balloons which have been known to explode when near only a very small cloud. Aeroplanes, gliders and boats can be bonded so that the crew have a Faraday cage. Buildings and boats can be fitted with lightning conductors – the sailing boat has one anyway in its mast – and can be earthed ('grounded' in the United States, though no one uses the term watered). Boats seem surprisingly safe. They do get struck, the discharge finds the quickest way to 'earth', which is by no means straight down an aluminium or wooden mast; wire shrouds and rigging are quicker. If the boat is anchored or moored mostly by chain, the forestay provides a handy lead. Damage to the boat is likely only where the current has had to make a few quick jumps over interruptions in its path.

Gliders are at risk from lightning strikes on two counts. If or when venturing into thunderstorms, and while being winch-launched. Climbing 1,000 ft high on a wire produces a super 1,000-ft lightning conductor and over the years a small number of gliders have been struck. The risk, however, is well known, and in any case is apparent, approaching rumbling thunderstorms being very obvious. The other risk, of being struck while flying inside the storm is also rare, because cu–nb flying is no longer as popular, or with increased controlled airspace, as possible as it once was. The danger is not so much one of being electrocuted as in having the glider damaged in a way that will cause subsequent failure. One of the features of this sort of strike is that the surface may have no more than a pin-hole mark, which is difficult to see. But inside, metal fittings or control cables may be fused or almost severed. If there is any suspicion of a strike a really thorough inspection is essential before the aircraft is flown again. And that applies to boats, too.

Fire and electricity can cause accidents very easily. But they are, in reality, finite simple things, and trouble from them can be avoided by simple, straightforward means. They are not variables like a person's judgement or forgetfulness. The risks need to be known, and treated with respect. Longstops, like extinguishers, need to be available, serviceable, and their operation understood. There is no need to add fire or explosion to all the other less easily avoidable hazards.

By now the wind was gusting force 9 and even in the river there was a steep chop as the flood-tide met the gale. The little 12-hp engine could not cope with the boat's windage coupled with the stopping effect of the short waves. It was difficult to keep the boat's head into it, and even when this was possible she made no progress. They were being quickly set on to the lee side of the channel, so he swung her hard to starboard, hoping that there was room to turn. She thumped once on the mud and came off, just giving the skipper time to do what he should have done before – reset the close-reefed mainsail. With this she became balanced and he was able to motor tack up the channel.

Upwind the sky was black, but there seemed just enough time to winch launch the two-seat glider for one more circuit on this short, cold, winter afternoon. About half-way up the launch, at some 500 ft, the glider flew suddenly into snow and the ground disappeared totally. The instructor released the cable at once and tried to get his airspeed right, and without instruments make some sort of a turn to stay within reach of the landing field and retain control. The black shape that flashed past was part of the roof of the hangar, but it was enough to help him with both immediate objectives. He turned a bit more, then straightened up and almost at once landed hard on the tussocky grass.

The Problems

Most weather-related accidents happen because, although the weather is around all the time, its behaviour is not observed or understood well enough. There are several reasons why the weather can become a problem:

It is unsuitable for the intended undertaking;

It becomes unsuitable after the undertaking has begun;

The skill and experience of the operator is insufficient and/or the equipment is inadequate to cope with the expected range of weather;

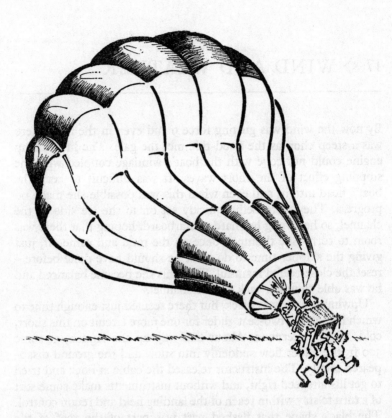

The weather also causes conditions on the surface to become unsuitable; e.g., big waves, flooding potholes, dust-storms.

Most people become conditioned to living their lives in the mostly moderate temperature and weather of their homeland, and become good at protecting themselves from any excesses it may display. Houses, clothes, food, bus shelters, hours of work, even street cleaning are arranged to suit. Although this is desirable it also has the effect of creating a somewhat negative approach to the weather. It is only when people involve themselves with flying or in going into or under the water and *have* to stay out in it, that they discover that a much more positive attitude is demanded. It is no longer a matter of taking a raincoat or sunhat just in case, or sheltering in a shop entrance from a sudden squall. You are in the weather, it is obviously getting worse, and you, and only you, can

now protect yourself from its fury. What is done and whether it avoids disaster or speeds its arrival depends on how well the behaviour of the weather is understood.

For some reason, perhaps because meteorology so often seems to be taught in a complicated or over-theoretical manner, many people are scared off learning, deciding that 'It is all too difficult, and anyway there are plenty of forecasts.' As a result too many people launch themselves off into the elements without much idea of what the weather is doing, and without knowing how to interpret the changes in the appearance of the sky that take place in front of their own eyes.

Sports vary widely not only in their weather requirements but in their sensitivity to it. Hot-air balloons may become unlaunchable in a fresh breeze because they turn themselves into spinnakers instead of containers; yachts prefer moderate winds, yet have to be capable of riding out a whole gale because they cannot get off the sea when it arrives. Hang gliders simply go backwards into the bushes if the wind is stronger than their low flying speed. Gliders require thermal upcurrents to fulfil their purpose, and mountaineers and potholers do not need too much rain. Light aeroplanes can do without fog, low cloud, falling snow or big thunderstorms. They do not have to take off in bad conditions and because of their speed have a good diversion capability, but they can also be caught out equally quickly.

In accident reports of those who have somehow failed to cope with the weather in which they found themselves, there is invariably the statement that 'a forecast had been obtained'. It is as though the act of reading, listening to, or writing down a chunk of information is a sort of sure-fire insurance policy, instead of merely the bare bones on which working weather assessment is made; a sort of guideline from which to observe and calculate what is actually happening outside. However accurate a forecast may seem, or turns out to be, it should only be used as such, and never as data requiring no further expenditure of effort.

Learning about Weather

Shortfalls in the understanding of weather problems are perhaps threefold: not knowing how to interpret the forecast obtained; not knowing what to look for in the sky to see how the weather is changing; and insufficient knowledge of the basic physics needed to work out what will be the effect of changes observed.

The problem with learning more about the weather is to know where to start. The need is not to become a professional meteorologist capable of making long-term forecasts, but to learn how to get a very good idea indeed of the weather that will turn up within the next few hours, in the intended area of operation, so that correct decisions can be taken in time. This is primarily a matter of observation linked to a few simple principles. If, for example, the pressure is falling this means that air is spreading out, mostly upwards. Air that rises for any reason cools. Cool air is less able to carry as much invisible water vapour as when it is warm, so as the rising, expanding air cools some moisture will be condensed out into tiny water drops. These droplets are cloud. When, therefore, the barometer or the forecaster indicates that pressure is falling an increase in cloud in one form or another *will* occur. This increase in cloud may merely reduce the amount of heating reaching the surface, so that the climber is colder or the glider pilot has his thermals spoilt, or it may continue to thicken until it gives rain. Conversely, when the pressure rises there will be some overall reduction in the amount or thickness of the cloud.

The need to know how much wind is going to turn up is an important factor in most outdoor activities, particularly if it is likely to get strong. Wind is simply air moving from regions of higher pressure to where it is lower; the greater the fall of pressure over a given distance the stronger the wind. Whenever the barometric pressure is seen or is forecast to be changing rapidly the wind should be expected to increase. After a cold front has gone through and the sky has become clear and blue, strong winds should be anticipated because the higher pressure behind the cold front is still hastening after the lower-pressure warm front. If a depression bumps up against an established anticyclone the air flowing between the two will be squeezed, and the wind become strong. On the weather chart this will be shown by the closeness of the lines of equal pressure, the isobars. Sea-breezes are caused when the land and the air over it is heated on a summer day; this warmed air becomes less dense and rises, and the cooler, denser, sea air flows landward to reduce the developing pressure difference.

Recognising What is Seen

Starting with this simple approach the intelligent observer of the weather will discover that with practice he can become quite good, not only at avoiding being caught out, but at using the weather to his positive advantage. The pilot, flying home late on a still winter afternoon, will know that the surface is cooling and he will anticipate ground-fog. The small-boat sailor will know that the strengthening wind will also kick up a steep sea and cause his boat to move less efficiently through the water. If he sees cumulus clouds growing over the land he will know that a sea-breeze may develop and can sail a course to enable him to take advantage of it.

Careful observation will soon provide the information that squalls and storms not only may grow in size as they approach, but also do not always move directly with the general wind. In the past a surprising number of square-rigged ships keeled over and sank when hit by a 'sudden' squall, which could only be ascribed to non-recognition or non-appreciation of the risk, as in European waters a developing unstable-air squall rarely gives less than about 20 min visual warning. Since sail changing on a square-rigger is a slow and laborious process, it is perhaps understandable that there would be considerable disinclination to have sails go up and down like yo-yos, but the alternative was sometimes costly.

The Mediterranean is notorious for the speed with which the wind and waves can rise, which sometimes adds an interesting dimension to the pressures of small-boat racing. One dinghy contest began in only a fresh breeze and a large but gentle swell, but this rapidly and unexpectedly changed to force 4–5; the reasonable upper limit for a well-sailed big dinghy. But since it was a race the boats kept going with crewmen out on their trapezes. One boat, near the head of the fleet, found itself almost becoming airborne off the crest of each wave, and each time it fell into the trough it did so hard. By now there was a great deal of water inside the boat, but it was managing to hold its position. As the wind rose through force 6, and the waves became overwhelming in size and steepness, the dinghy became increasingly difficult to steer. Bearing off on a beam reach with the crewman still out on the trapeze the dinghy shot off the top of an extra large wave, and then uncontrollably broached in the trough. No beginners, this pair, they regained control and went off on a wild plane seeing almost nothing through the spray. But such exhilarating transport could not be expected to last; it ended almost at once as the boat plummeted down the next wave face. The helmsman shouted for the crew to come in off his trapeze as they hit the back of the wave in front, and just drove right under. Surfacing on to the hull, the two had a look around to find that only four out of the seventy starters were still upright, and these were taking their sails down fast! The next few minutes were spent swimming in the now huge waves to try to get the sails off, so that there would be some chance of her staying upright when they tried to right her. But even this was frustrated as the hull all but sank with a gurgling noise. The loads on the upturned boat from the fierce sea had been enough to distort the hull and allow the buoyancy tank hatches to spring. An Italian fishing boat picked them up and towed the submerged hull back to the boat park, where it was added to the growing pile of wreckage. In less than 10 min the waves had gone from acceptable four-footers to 10–12 ft high.

Hazards at Sea

Although when racing, due to the proximity of other boats and organised rescue facilities, risks may be taken deliberately, every effort should be made to avoid adding to hazards of the sea which already exist, particularly when cruising alone and with a small crew. Understanding the weather is of primary importance, including study of these special weather problems that have a habit of predominating in their own localities. People intending to sail offshore anywhere from the Caribbean up to the eastern US seaboard or out into the Atlantic in late summer have to consider the hurricane risks long and earnestly before setting off. Boat-crews sailing off to the Canadian and Newfoundland coast would be unworldly if they did not prepare to work through sea fog, perhaps for days on end. Much useful information can be obtained from local people, although not every theory or hair-raising tale should be believed. For many sailors in Britain the English Channel between the Solent and the Channel Islands provides delightful cruising waters with many congenial ports and harbours. Most of the time the weather ranges from fine to merely tedious, whether it has been accurately forecast or not; but it is not so often dangerous without reasonable warning. But just occasionally it is, and for the same sort of reasons each time. The size and shape of the long Channel which is aligned approximately ENE – WSW contributes to the problem. If there is, for example, a NE wind blowing round an anticyclone over Britain and this wind aligns with the English Channel, it blows faster down its unobstructed length than might be expected from listening to the general forecasts. After a day or two of north-easters over the sea at the western end of the Channel, where the wind fetch is of the order of 250 miles, the sea swell may be much bigger than expected. If only the general forecasts (mostly intended for the land) are heard, about 1 force should automatically be added to the forecast wind speed.

A much more dangerous situation develops rapidly, and sometimes at the height of the sailing season, when a depression is moving ENE across Britain with fronts trailing down over the eastern Atlantic. Sometimes a small, fierce secondary depression develops on the trailing front. It is difficult to forecast, and moves rapidly up-channel, its circulation giving wind changes usually from SW right around the clock in the space of a few hours. These winds will be strong, perhaps gale force for short periods, and the accompanying weather is vile. Because little warning may be available, it is easy to be caught out too close to a lee shore for safety. Even in harbour there may be no guarantee of security.

On 5 July 1969 the barometer began falling over the Western Approaches, and the next forecast spoke of a depression moving up-channel (from SSW) at 30 knots. As a precaution, the crew of a small Ranger cruising boat on holiday, at Herm in the Channel Islands, decided to go to the more sheltered anchorage at Braye, in Alderney, as this gave good protection from SW–NW. Although the forecast had not mentioned winds, they reckoned that most would be westerly. In the early afternoon they anchored at Braye and were just preparing to go ashore when someone on a near-by boat shouted across that he had just heard an imminent (in less than 6 hrs) gale warning, wind expected force 9, *NE*. The trip to the pub was abandoned, and the boat secured in every possible way, because NE was the one direction in which Braye offers no shelter, and it was now not possible to depart for anywhere safer. By 20.00 hrs with the barometer still falling, the weather had really arrived. The sea was breaking green over the harbour wall, throwing up gravel and rocks, it was raining heavily, and several boats were already dragging their anchors. There were a lot of yachts in the little harbour that night, and now many of them were using their engines to motor slowly ahead into the wind to take some of the load off anchor chains and warps. At this moment the Ranger took off backwards travelling through the other boats as the anchor hold suddenly gave. Quickly starting the engine, which they had kept warm and ready, the crew motored out towards the harbour entrance. The wind and sea there were just as bad, but with more space around them it was possible to let out more cable. They now had 25 fathoms (150 ft) out. This was just as well, as not only were the gusts increasing, but with the tide now on the ebb, the boat was swinging in an arc of 180°. And at the end of each swing coming up with a fearful jolt, before charging off again like a maddened racehorse. It was not until 01.00 that there was any respite. Then the wind backed to N, so that the breakwater became more effective. At 04.30 the wind backed to NW, and although it was still blowing the crew were able to fall exhausted into their bunks. This little secondary depression took twenty-one lives.

Fog

Although excessive wind and its effect on the sea sets the scene for most boat accidents, another real bugbear is fog. There are various sorts of fog. On land radiation-fog occurs as a result of rapid cooling on a clear night, causing condensation in the damp air near the ground. Hill-fog exists when cloud is low enough to sit on hills, and sometimes even on low ground. Fog can also develop in anticyclonic haze conditions if the air is dirty enough. At sea, apart from hill-fog which can also lower itself to the sea surface as, for example, in the passage of a warm front, advection fog develops when there is considerable dissimilarity in the temperatures of the water and of the air passing over it. The famous Grand Banks fog is due to cold Arctic and near Arctic air flowing over the more northerly meanderings of the warmer Gulf Stream. Around the British coasts the sea-fogs that sometimes tediously develop during the summer holiday time are caused by very warm air moving over cool coastal waters. Sometimes these banks of fog merely lie some miles out to sea, but if a sea-breeze develops, and air is pulled in towards the land the sea-fog will roll in with it like an airborne tide. The problem with sea-fog, whether caused by frontal conditions, or by water/air temperature differences is that nothing is seen any more. This increases the chance of either getting lost or collision, or both.

Fog can be Expensive

In 1923 fourteen destroyers set off on high-speed trials along the coast of California. Steaming at 20 knots in columns three abreast, the intention was to go south and then turn east towards San Diego. Before the days of electronic navigation, the mist had made the taking of sun sights impossible. By 18.00 hrs the little fleet was not too sure of its exact position. Then the lead destroyer obtained a single radio bearing from a shore station which tied in with the dead reckoning position. It was accepted as confirmation, in spite of the usual suspicion with which radio bearings were regarded at that time. The radio bearing was, in fact, correct although the ships were closer inshore than calculated. Subsequent radio bearings which showed the ships close to land were ignored because the navigator on the lead destroyer was considered to be infallible (and was also the top navigating instructor at the navy academy). At 21.00 the left turn was ordered and all the destroyers swung round on to a heading of 095 degrees, except the leader of one column, whose misgivings about position were strong enough for him to take the serious step of disobeying an order. He had also recently been reprimanded by the Commodore, and his sulky mood may have contributed to his unilateral action.

Within 10 min of the lead destroyer turning she ran into a thick bank of fog, and almost immediately into rocks at the foot of Honda Point. Although the ship was wrecked the first thought was to warn those astern by broadcasting a message for all ships to turn west. Lights were also turned on and whistles blown. They then went full astern on their engines, kicking up a white froth of sea. This was the first sign of any difficulty to the next ship astern as she arrived, still doing 20 knots. The master swung hard left, missed the lead destroyer and promptly went into the rocks. The third ship bounced over submerged rocks, ripped out most of her port side and sank. Then the next ship hit. The three ships in the next column appeared on a scene of total confusion, but going too fast to stop, so added themselves to the now enormously expensive pile of wreckage. It was incredible that only twenty-three people were killed.

These crews were no weekend amateurs, but highly disciplined with all the aids and expertise of the time available to them. Aids, in fact, that are just about the equivalent of what many small-boat sailors have today; with the same pride, complacency and over-confidence just as available.

The coastguard once got a radio call from a boat which had suddenly gone aground in fog, with the skipper so sure he was in deep water he had not turned on his echo-sounder. He told them he was aground on the Farne Islands in thick fog and what should he do. To give any sort of sensible answer the coastguard needed to know exactly which of the little islands he was on, so they asked him what he could see. An irritated voice replied that he could see bloody nothing – it was foggy, remember. Then there was a pause, and he added 'But I can hear a train.' The coastguard breathed a sigh of relief or exasperation. The boat could be aground in only one place, and that was on the mainland coast, many miles from the islands.

Collision in Fog

Collision is the real risk in fog, because even with care it cannot always be avoided. Fog is usually, but not always, associated with light winds, when a small sailing boat is not always in the best situation to move out of the way. If the engine is run the other vessel will probably not be heard until it is too close to avoid. Large ships may not notice the little paint of a radar reflector, or may not be looking that closely. Transponders are not only expensive but their wholesale use would be chaotic. So collision in fog at sea is a real and frightening risk for any small boat. It is even more alarming when your boat is actually cut in half, as happened to a 7-ton motor sailor making for Cherbourg with a crew of two.

As they approached, the fog that had been intermittent across the Channel thickened, so they decided not to attempt to enter the harbour until after dark when the enormously powerful guide lights would have been turned on. Later and after one unsuccessful try they went back out to sea again, and having been up for 22 hrs took it in turns to get some sleep. At 02.00 they were just

changing over when a ship appeared making straight for them. They switched on a powerful lamp that they had kept in readiness to supplement the navigation lights, and blasted hopefully on their fog-horn. Their radar reflector was still properly positioned high in the rigging. All to no avail. The ship kept coming. It sliced through the motor sailor just forward of the mast, and noisily vanished on its way. The two crew, although knocked down by the impact, were not hurt, but the boat quickly sank. Frantically they abandoned ship into the inflatable, which had been kept partially inflated, together with a pump, flares, a wet blanket, and anything else that could be grabbed in passing. Then they were bobbing about in the fog, without food or water in the middle of the night. It was difficult to know whether to start rowing for France or England, so great was the confusion of thought that inflicts itself in such an abrupt change of circumstance. But the sea was fairly smooth and after a while the fog thinned. In sight was a fishing boat. They fired a flare which scattered burning bits on to the rubber dinghy but failed to alert the fishing boat crew. Two hours later an Italian tanker with a Greek crew stopped in response to their next pyrotechnic display. The captain said he would be delighted to rescue them. He was short of crew, and was on his way to Italy direct. Their hearts sank. Work demanded their presence on Monday morning and not in a week or so's time. Maybe it was the events of the night that had dislocated their assessment of priorities, but it somehow seemed better to stay in the dinghy. The Captain asked in disbelief if they 'reely wanted to getta back into *that*', arranged over the radio for aid to come to their position, and heaped on them some food. Dawn found them still bobbing about, realising they must be crazy, and staring with dismay at three frozen loaves of bread, a $2\frac{1}{2}$-lb cheese, twelve tins of sardines and corned beef, a huge chunk of frozen pears, cigarettes, six bottles of Coke and one of whisky. The captain's last words had been 'Justa stay where you are.' But now a wind started up blowing them across the water, so they kept trying to row back to the same position, until they realised it was no longer possible to know if this was in fact what they were doing. Then they just sat, conserved their energy and ate the thawing edges of the pears. At 15.30 a navy ship, diverted to search from its gunnery trials, decided to return home having found nothing. It was hopeless wasting more time until the fog lifted. So they emptied the hot baths they had run for shipwrecked mariners and set off. Then on their radar they spotted something. It was the errant inflatable, and after 14 hrs in the dinghy the two were picked up. The ship, *Decoy*, had often been sent on searches in the past, but as this was the first time they had actually found anything it called for a celebration.

Frontal Fog

The fog that causes most problems for both mountaineers and pilots is that which clamps itself on to hills and mountains in frontal situations. Being lost in fog on hills or mountains often results in complete bewilderment and consequent chaos, if the walker or climber blunders on hoping soon to see something that is recognisable. With small aeroplanes the risk is flying unwittingly into high ground, radio masts, or – if the fog and disorientation are severe enough – even flat ground. The aeroplane cannot stop until it is on the surface, and the difficulty is to get there; unable to travel slowly the hazard turns up with minimal warning, even none at all. Also the circumstances producing frontal hill-fog are invariably associated with falling air pressure, and aeroplane altimeters are pressure-reading instruments. The pressure of the air over the surface of the earth falls with height and this is presented on altimeters in terms of feet, or metres, of height, based on a norm of 1013.2 mb. When the air pressure falls below the norm, as in the passage of a frontal trough, the air is 'thinned out'. The altimeter will therefore show a greater altitude than actually exists. A pilot without radio is on his own, and when flying low in deteriorating weather must assume that his altimeter will over-read, and allow for it. The same is true, of course, for the hill walker. If he carries a pocket altimeter and is relying on this to help him navigate his way down a mountain in frontal trough weather, he must expect to be lower than his altimeter indicates, and may not, therefore, be where he thought he was.

Frontal-trough hill-fog approaches insidiously because the weather usually deteriorates only slowly. When starting off on the climb, or flight, there may be complete overcast, but with a marked cloud-base and perfectly clear air with reasonable visibility underneath. But as a front approaches the cloud gradually thickens and its base gently lowers until it reaches the ground. The lowering cloud base becomes increasingly indistinct, and maybe accompanied by slight mizzle or drizzle, which masks it even more. Quite suddenly, sometimes even unexpectedly, it reaches the level of the operator, and he is in the fog. The climber can probably stop and consider, but this is number one killer for the cross-country light aeroplane.

A few years ago three young pilots wanted to visit a flying display at Shobden in Hereford in a Tripacer. They were not very experienced, but had been taught to prepare and plan a flight with care. None had instrument flying experience. The forecast they obtained warned of a warm front over Devon, a cold front farther away over Cornwall, with a shallow depression running east into the Bristol Channel; all to the west and towards their intended destination. The wind at 2,000 ft was expected to increase to SW 30 knots, with cloud increasing to 8/8, and lower to 1,500 ft with rain as they went west. Their destination forecast mentioned rain with visibility down to 4 km, plus some cloud as low as 800 ft. Having some doubts about the suitability of this weather, the three planned to go via Staverton airfield where they could land and recheck the destination weather. They landed, and in addition to getting the Met information, arranged for Staverton to give them radio headings, if they needed to turn back. Ten minutes after take-off they called Shobden, but apparently could not hear them answer. About this time the aeroplane was noticed by someone on the ground at Leominster to come out of the cloud, circle as though the pilot was trying to identify something, fly away, return and circle, and then fly away again. Shortly after it was seen by someone else flying very low, in a direction which was away from their destination. It could be that they had confused Leominster with Hereford, not all that difficult in the circumstances. Soon after, in cloud, they flew into a 950-ft hill 5 miles NE of their destination and were killed.

Luck can Help

Sometimes, although not too often, luck, our old friend random chance, puts in an appearance. Another pilot departed from Wales to fly to the Isle of Wight. On the way cloud steadily descended and at one time over the Wiltshire Downs the pilot was bumbling along at only 200 ft. Having a feeling that the weather would be all right at Sandown on the island, an optimism that is occasionally justified if you understand the local weather, he pressed on across the Solent – now flying at only 50 ft! But he had a plan – to fly around the not very large island and attack Sandown from the sea; but then he reckoned he could cut the corner and go in to the land more directly. Almost instantly the drizzle became cloud, with forward visibility nil. With no time to look at instruments he was still looking out when the cloud ahead went dark. The pilot turned steeply. The undercarriage hit the hill face and collapsed. The aeroplane then careered and slithered down the steep side of the hill and fetched up at the bottom, facing the way it had come. The pilot and passenger climbed out with only a few bruises between them.

Instruments or Eyes

There are only two ways of flying with reasonable safety in this sort of weather: (a) on instruments, with navigational aids and in contact with air traffic control and their radar facilities: to do this it is necessary to be experienced, competent, and have current practice in the use of these aids; (b) to fly contact, under cloud, *never* go into it, and turn back in time. For this experience is also needed, with different skills, as well as the cunning of the hunted. There are no half-measures, and almost no second chances. Pride, a brand-new instrument rating, memories of past skills, absence of imagination, and hope are all non-solutions.

Change: Unexpected and Fast

Although weather may seem to change very rapidly if it is flown into at 160 knots or so, over flatlands or the sea it does not actually change that fast. Warnings of its arrival can be seen by the observant. This is not always so in the mountains, because it is sometimes the massif itself which accelerates the weather deterioration. A simple increase in wind strength, for example, causes changes in the airflow pattern, and if this involves any increased upward deflection, which it probably will, the air locally will be quickly further cooled. If this air is also moist the cooling will produce cloud; not above, but all around. This may not only be sudden and all-enveloping, but will also drop the temperature by cutting off the warmth of the sun.

It was such an unexpected weather change that probably caused the death of a 1975 Everest climber. Two had just reached the summit and were starting down when they met another of the team. He was a very experienced climber, and wanted them to return to the summit so that he could photograph them. They declined, being already roped up for descent, and went on down. They were not worried about their companion, expected him to go up the short distance on good snow to the top up the fixed rope, and then follow them down. They arranged to meet at the big rock of the S Summit.

But almost as soon as they left him the local weather changed. There had been high cloud earlier with visibility steadily worsening, but now cloud with whirling snow was suddenly all around them. The sky and the mountain merged together, visibility dropped to 3 m and tracks vanished. The two reached the rock with some difficulty and waited as agreed. After 1½ hrs they could do so no longer; even getting themselves down would now be marginal. The route and the fixed ropes were almost impossible to find in the snow as it was now also dark. On the way they were covered by two powder-snow avalanches that they could not see coming. One of them lost a crampon on a traverse and the other fell to the end of his rope down a rock slope. One of the fixed ropes had been swept away. They arrived at their camp tent at 19.30, and were pinned there for two nights and a day, getting frostbite in the process.

Certainly people who venture on mountains like Everest do so with their eyes open and with great experience and courage, but the weather can be a relentless adversary. The more challenging the moment in time the greater the vigilance and comprehension needed.

Ice and Icing

As altitude is gained the temperature falls between 1.5° in cloud and 3 °C in clear air per 1,000 ft. Even on a summer day, when it is warm at the surface, freezing and icing conditions are readily to hand, maybe less than a mile away in a vertical sense. The problem of cold to a person on a hill or mountain is straightforward provided he does not get lost, because it is not difficult to prepare for whatever expedition is intended. To aeroplane and glider pilots cold as such is not too much of a problem either. What does create a less desirable situation is the aircraft icing that goes with it. This may prevent the aircraft taking off, severely reduce its performance if it occurs in the air, cause engine failure through ice forming in the carburettor intake, result in no airspeed indicator readings, make the windscreen opaque, or all of these at the same time. What may seem unexpected about aircraft icing is that the risk exists only in the clouds comprised of water droplets, and not in ice crystal clouds. And that although ice thaws at 0 °C, water droplets may not freeze until the temperature is as low as −10 °C. The droplets just sit around supercooled in clouds until an aeroplane or glider comes rushing through. They then freeze on to the aircraft, building a coating of ice on projecting surfaces, leading edges, canopies and elsewhere. If the temperature is low, close to −10 °C, the ice accumulation will be small, because the vapour is just about ready to turn itself into ice crystals anyway. If the cloud is warmer a much higher quantity of water droplets will be available to freeze on to the cold aircraft. And the longer the aircraft stays in this sort of wet cloud in an air temperature a little under freezing the more ice will accumulate. Freezing rain, outside of cloud, produces icing if the air and aircraft temperature are below freezing. If an aircraft becomes loaded with ice, its weight increases and so does its stalling speed. The performance of a glider will deteriorate and it will go less far from any given height, and an aeroplane will need more power to achieve a given speed or rate of climb; and this it may not have. Since airframe icing is most likely to occur between air temperatures of 0 °C and 10° C, changing altitude, either up to colder, drier, air where no more ice will grow, or down to warmer levels where it will melt, is the best way to reduce the problem. What is possible will, of course, depend on the circumstances at the time, particularly if there is insufficient terrain clearance to permit a safe descent. Because ice thaws at a higher temperature than it freezes it may seem to take an excessively long time to melt. If the ice appeared on the wings at, say, 7,000 ft, the aircraft could be several thousand feet lower before it disappears. This can be very tedious if the windscreen is covered; the aircraft may have come out of cloud but the pilot still not be able to see anything.

Ice on Take-off

Whereas accumulating ice in flight may be unavoidable, taking off, or rather attempting to do so, with any ice at all on the wings, is a sure way to calamity. During the war a formation of Magisters took off at dawn. Not one made it above 50 ft and they fell all over the place, one going through a bungalow roof, and fetching up on the breakfast table. The reason was a very thin coating of overnight frost on the wings, giving them a sandpaper surface unlike anything the designer had intended.

Whiteout and Depth Perception

Another serious, and sometimes unexpected problem is whiteout, when there are large expanses of featureless snow. This inhibits depth perception so that the pilot has no idea how high he is above the surface. One pilot flying in the Arctic on a day of poor visibility noticed his airspeed indicator needle creeping backwards. To avoid stalling he added some power and moved the stick forward, but relentlessly the needle went on retreating until it reached the zero stop. Thoroughly confused by thoughts of mechanical and electrical failure, it took the pilot several seconds to realise that it was not the ASI needle, but the whole aeroplane which was now no longer moving. As the engines choked to death he discovered that they had quietly submerged in deep soft snow.

Depth perception departs as well when over glassy-water lakes, or occasionally even over the sea. At one time pilots were told that when parachuting into water they should release the harness at 10 ft or so above the surface, to reduce the risk of entanglement. But some pilots did this as high as 100 ft and others were found to have hit the water before they realised they were anywhere near the surface, because of this complete loss of depth perception when the surface is smooth and constant, and when there are no other objects or differences to relate to. With a small aeroplane, land or float, about the only secure way to overcome the problem is for the pilot to use a suitable combination of speed and power to give about a 200 ft per min rate of descent. This brings the aeroplane on to the surface in a reasonable landing altitude. A glider, except in the unlikely event of a strong wind, should be brought in at an approach speed which is just a little on the slow side, with $\frac{1}{2}$ to $\frac{1}{3}$ airbrake held steadily in this position.

Anticipating the Weather

The need, with all weather problems is to know in advance what to expect: to understand the weather and its habits, and what it looks like, well enough so that the risk of being caught out by it is minimal. To sit in the air wondering why the engine power is fading is not the time to start learning about the sort of conditions that are fine for carburettor icing. To wait for the calm of the evening is not the time to start to do a first floatplane landing nor is potholing always sensible with thunderstorms forecast. Some pilots seem to think that a thunderstorm is something that can be flown around – and often it is. But if the instability is right for the formation of thunderstorms why should there be only one? Thunderstorms can develop simultaneously and spontaneously all over the sky if conditions are right. Then there is no way round to go. In the United States where thunderstorms are much more ferocious than are usual in Europe, pilots are killed every year because they either do not know, or will not recognise, this one fact.

Inside Thunderstorms

Once inside a thunderstorm problems are handed out freely. As well as icing, there can be blinding rain, wing-denting hail, lightning, and vicious turbulence. In the earlier days of gliding, before atmospheric waves were discovered, pilots wanting to go high used cu-nb. They became highly skilled at doing battle with these giants, but there were also accidents when the glider structure failed. Usually there was not too much difficulty getting free of the aircraft; and parachutes had been reliable for a long time. But there were other problems; the most dramatic being caused by the immense power of the upcurrents in big cumulonimbus clouds, 65 ft per sec being not unusual. A parachute descends at 16 ft per second, and the sort of height that the glider would be finally overwhelmed would probably be 10,000 ft or above. The turbulence would be disorientating and tiring to the pilot and the glider would be accumulating more and more ice. A pilot baling out at around 15,000 ft would hope to go down, not up. But caught in the updraught he would not only be carried up still higher, but for long enough to freeze him to death, because the outside air temperature on a summer day would be down to freezing at about 10,000 ft, down to −30 °C at 20,000 ft and −45 °C at 25,000 ft. It seems scarcely sporting that at the same time as being deep-frozen, the pilot also carried the risk of being struck by lightning.

In the last international gliding championships before the Second World War a large thunderstorm, with its enticement to record heights caused three such deaths. Two pilots were glaciated and one incinerated. To avoid future disasters of this sort some pilots decided that rather than end this way, should they be unfortunate to have their newer stronger gliders break up, they would delay opening their parachute until they reckoned that the risk was sufficiently reduced. This presupposed that the bale-out height was known, which was not always the case. One pilot turned face up during the free fall, and with heavy rain hitting his eyes at 65 knots could not see anything; not even when he came through the bottom of the cloud and shortly afterwards hit the ground. Although glider flying in thunderclouds is now rare the problem remains for any pilot needing to depart from his aircraft in a thunderstorm.

Man-made Turbulence

As if natural forces were not enough to have to deal with, additional upset is created by man with the wake turbulence of aircraft and washes and wakes from boats. The care needed when following a big aircraft into land, if the little fellow is not to be rolled over is now well understood, although it still continues to happen. The main offenders are the vortices which trail from each wingtip, spiralling as they go. They increase in size with distance from the aircraft but only slowly weaken. In extreme cases wake turbulence may be felt 5–6 miles astern. As would be expected the disturbed wake gradually sinks or descends and is also drifted on the wind, so it should be expected lower and downwind of the aircraft causing it. Helicopters produce considerable turbulence, particularly downward while hovering. Hang gliders, which have a large wing area and fly slowly at a high angle of attack, create wakes sufficient to make a following hang glider difficult to control. Gliders, although flying in close proximity in thermals, are very clean in shape and do not create a problem.

Although man can produce disturbing turbulence or informative contrails he is in no position to ameliorate the weather's bad habits. Not only is there no possibility of changing the weather to suit; there is often no means of escaping from it either. The only way of coming to terms with it is to understand it. Every change in the weather is clearly heralded in the changing appearance of the clouds, or lack of them, and in the behaviour of the wind. There is a need to learn to look.

Last summer, off the rocky and treacherous north coast of Cornwall, a beachguard heard cries for help from the fog-shrouded sea. He swam through the gentle surf and on out for 100 yds or so, when he came upon a large cruising catamaran ghosting along under sail. One of the crew shouted 'Which way to Padstow?' The lifeguard, swallowing a mouthful of water in astonishment, closely followed by irritation, pointed the direction. Thanks, called the crew, and the boat vanished in the fog.

Whether it arrived safely or not is immaterial, but something like half the boats which go aground away from their own home waters do so because the crew thinks that they are somewhere else. One small tanker went ashore on the south Devon coast a few years ago, where it was seen by a passer-by who felt there was something familiar about it. Then he remembered that some days before he had seen her stranded on the shore in south Wales. A Gallic crabber hit the bottom of 200-ft Devon cliffs, and the first thing the crew knew that they were anywhere dangerous was when the glasses flew off the table, as the boat came to an abrupt stop. A £25,000 yacht drawing 6 ft of water arrived in Salcombe recently, the crew calling across to ask how far they could go up the 'river', pointing to a dead-end creek. They had come 250 miles from the Kent coast, but had no charts this far west. An expensive and fully equipped motor cruiser became 'lost' in the North Sea and called the coastguard on the radio for help. The crew was asked to get out their charts so they could be told what to do and what to look for. When they replied asking if the chart was 'that map with the funny little numbers all over it', the coastguard sighed deeply, and sent out the lifeboat to escort them back to civilisation. But no one can say that they have never been lost at one time or another. Maybe the occasion was merely tedious, like driving about for an hour in a maze of country lanes, or maybe it was dangerous, like missing the path on empty moorland on a cold winter afternoon, but everyone has done it. There are many reasons for getting lost: failing to walk, fly, or sail in a straight line, or keep track of time and distance; not having an accurate compass or not knowing how to use one; failing to obtain the available information from a map or chart, or feeling under-confident about sense of direction. There is also failure to appreciate the effects of moving in more than one direction at the same time, as when influenced by tidal streams or wind drift in the air. Yet all these basic navigational and orienteering skills are as necessary as a spade is to a gardener.

If becoming lost is to be avoided it is necessary to know the destination; the direction in which it lies; how long it should take to get there; and along the way it is necessary to keep track of progress made.

How to get Lost – or Not

It is keeping track which produces most problems; a great deal of work is put into the planning of the trip or cruise, the navigation is well organised, charts or maps are suitable and the compass accurate. The voyage begins well enough, and then the system is allowed to fall apart. There seem to be no navigational problems, time passes, excuses are made for the absence of features expected to be seen – or there is conviction that what is seen is what is supposed to be seen. Suddenly you are lost. In the effort to find yourself other things go wrong because concentration is now devoted to this single difficulty, and all else is forgotten. In a light aeroplane it is usually the fuel check that is not made, and the pilot runs out of petrol on one tank, or even altogether, in his hopeful searchings for something familiar. Keeping meticulous track of position at regular intervals is the only safeguard against becoming lost. Even if the exact location at any given moment is not known, the pinpoint of 20 min earlier exists.

Writing down positions with the time is normal practice at sea. Many pilots do it in the air, but it is not so often practised by people walking on hills; yet in the sudden loss of visibility produced by snow, fog, or even darkness it may be the only means of avoiding a cold night out. The speed of walking, or the wind drift, or the tidal offset can all be roughly calculated so that the estimated distance covered and direction made good should not be too far out. If such checks are not made at intervals becoming unlost is much more difficult, because there is no recent checkpoint from which to sort out the navigation; and the longer the interval the larger the area of uncertainty.

Becoming Unlost

The worst thing that the operator can do when the sinking feeling comes to him that he has no longer any idea of where he has got to is to wander vaguely about, whether on foot or in an aircraft. The only thing to do is to stop, heave-to or anchor if at sea, and circle around a prominent landmark when flying. The time should be noted and full consideration given to what can be seen, its direction, and how far away it is. In the air and at sea more distant, and probably more prominent, landmarks are usually better to identify and relate to than endeavouring to make a jigsaw puzzle out of some straggly town below, or a jumble of similar-looking cliffs.

When something identifiable has been noted the need is to establish the relationship between it and the operator. This can be done either by taking a compass bearing, or assessing its direction in relation to the sun, and drawing the appropriate line on the map. If this process is repeated using a couple more distant landmarks the collection of lines drawn should hopefully cross, or nearly so, at some point. This is the area in which the operator probably is, and it will now be more profitable to attempt to identify nearer objects, because the choice has been limited. At sea the general position can often be verified by using the echo-sounder to check on the depth of water under the boat. If in no case does the closer landmark or the depth confirm the broader estimate of position, the process should be started all over again; the lost operator must never persuade himself on insufficient evidence that he is now found. This may require great self-honesty as the feeling of disorientation and confusion when utterly lost is considerable. It is remarkably easy to look at some unique and outstandingly prominent feature, although maybe from an unusual angle, and blankly fail to recognise it for what it is.

Eye Transits

Transits are an even simpler way of producing a collection of lines to cross on a general position. No compass is required because each line is produced from the alignment of two features, such as a distant peak and a village church in a nearer valley, or at sea the alignment of a distant headland and a navigational buoy. Almost since the beginning of time fishermen have used this method to find lobster pots or harbour entrance channels in poor visibility. Transits are also the simplest way of checking that an anchored boat is not dragging. If two transits are noted, say a white house with the end of the harbour wall, and at about 90° difference in direction a beach shop and a red buoy, and these remain steady, the boat is not moving. Transits should be taken as a matter of course by anyone in charge of a diving boat, not only when it is anchored, but whenever it is moved to another position.

Using a Compass

The compass is a basic tool, cheap and easily available, but it is a symptom of the dependent society that a very large number of people have never used one. Practice in orientation and direction-keeping are essential to any venturing on the sea or into the air, and the ability to read a compass properly should be possessed before embarking on such activities. It may seem to be bordering on the eccentric to carry a compass when horse riding on the sands, but when sea-fog suddenly rolled in on to a beach near the Humber

Estuary, followed rapidly by the tide, only one pony survived out of five riders and their mounts.

But the compass is also a good means of getting lost if it is not reading correctly, because someone left a camera light-meter or a pair of pliers near it, or because variation – the magnetic divergence of the needle from the north – was either forgotten about or applied incorrectly. If a compass is suspect, or even if it is not, the first part of any voyage or cross-country flight should be used to check the compass heading against surface features. The glider pilot, who spends much of his time circling in thermals with the compass needle trailing around after him, quickly develops the habit of setting off in the right direction in relation to a good distant landmark; and then checking what the compass is indicating. This disposes of most of the problems associated with compass errors and human miscalculations, including the most common one of all: flying the opposite way – 180° out in direction! Obviously, a compass should be maintained so that it is as accurate as reasonably possible, particularly if a long voyage is contemplated; but there is never harm in checking it by the practical means of going visually in the intended direction and then reading what the compass actually says. If it is possible for an airline pilot to have flown half-way across the Sahara in the wrong direction – until a passenger asked a steward why the sun was rising in the west, or for a pilot starting from Havana in a tiny 50-hp aeroplane to fetch up 270 miles away at Cat Cay in the Bahamas instead of his destination of Key West, Florida, 120 miles away – then no aids to navigational accuracy should be spurned.

As with bad weather poor navigation is not always the only failure needed to produce the accident. If the operator has already made another mistake, getting lost will contribute heartily towards the downward spiral, but if the navigational error was the first mistake others will follow easily because of the single-minded concentration needed to become unlost. One evening a well-found 32-ft yacht set off from near Southampton for Cherbourg. Approaching the coast around 04.00 visibility fell to only a few hundred yards in mist and drizzle. The crew had not kept track of the exact position of the yacht because until the unexpected weather deterioration, no problem of location on this well-lighted coast had been anticipated. The crew of three immediately turned the boat around and stood out to sea in safe water. About 20 min later the local weather improved and the boat returned landward looking for shore lights that would establish their position. Without warning, breakers appeared ahead. The boat was immediately put about, but at the same time it touched bottom. The crew rushed to lower sail, but even before they could do so the boat was thumped and lifted and thumped again hard. Waves began to break over her as she lay on her beam ends. Still not knowing where they were, or even how far distant the shore was the crew put on their life-jackets, and signalled mayday over the radio. No reply was received, and it was assumed the set could have been damaged by crashing about in the surf. Six distress flares were then fired but they produced no response either.

The next action was to get the dinghy out of the cockpit locker, but they had never attempted this previously at such an angle of heel with waves breaking over them, and it demanded almost superhuman effort. When at last they got it inflated and into the water it was immediately swamped. With two of them hanging on to it, the third crew member tried to bale it out. Suddenly an extra powerful wave pulled it out of their hands, and it disappeared into the darkness taking one crewman with it. In the stress of the moment they had failed to take the elementary precaution of using that ancient aid, a length of rope. With potential disaster growing by the minute the remaining crew threw *both* lifebuoys after it, complete with their flashing lights. Remarkably, this somewhat improvident act later proved valuable. At the time, however, the two remaining crew found themselves with no further aids to survival other than their personal life-jackets. The boat was now hammering on rocks so hard that it seemed as though it must soon break up, so the only alternative seemed to be abandon ship. Logical thought was now taking on an intermittent quality. They went into the water aiming to keep together, but were almost at once separated when one decided that he would prefer, after all, to stay with his ship, and in any case he had lost his glasses and could not see well enough where he was going. This vision problem also applied to his return to the boat, which, he now could not find among the big waves. So he swam about, swallowing water, his thoughts wandering from unhappiness over the loss of his yacht, to his own imminent demise from drowning. He began to hear strange voices. Luck took a hand at this moment in that he had somehow arrived near the dinghy. Both crew were now in it and shouting for him. The lifebuoy lights were winking away. He took a few moments to try to more calmly recover his breath, and then swam to the dinghy. At first the crew shouted at him to stay in the sea, as there was already too much of it inside the dinghy. But thinking more clearly now he reckoned that by climbing aboard he would displace quite a lot of ocean, so he got in.

When leaving the yacht the lights had been left on as a guide to possible rescuers, although the crew were, of course, now no longer there. As they watched the sad and distant glow they realised that the yacht had now refloated. Frantically they tried to get back to it, paddling with their hands and the one oar that had not been lost. Then the yacht went aground again. As dawn broke they paddled forlornly ashore. The tide ebbed away and they found the yacht on her side in the sand of a small bay. It was her sound construction that resulted in the damage being remarkably light. There were deep scores in the glass-fibre hull, but after first-aid repairs the crew sailed her home.

Stay Put until Sure

Happenings like that one reinforce the need, when lost, or even when the position is uncertain, to stay put; or immediately move to somewhere safer and stay there until it is possible to find out exactly how to get unlost. This crew having sensibly returned to seaward on first encountering the drizzly mist, should have stayed at sea until they could obtain enough *real evidence* to establish their exact position, before making any further attempts to reach the land. Contributory errors of this sort are made almost daily by people walking and scrambling about on hills, mountains, and cliffs. Hundreds of sorties are made by the coastguard and by rescue helicopters to retrieve such situations each year. The pattern is depressingly similar. Someone becomes lost, either through simply not keeping track of his position – 'I thought there would be a path', or 'I only took a little short cut', or because darkness fell, hill-fog enveloped him, or it started to snow. Although visibility remains not too unreasonable in rain, however heavy, it drops quite suddenly to almost nothing in falling snow. Because hills and mountains are higher than the flat land around the air is colder up there; so rain in the valley is no guarantee that there will not be snow higher up. Too often the first reaction of a person feeling lost in such circumstances is the near panic one of blundering off hopefully in some unthought-out direction; even the simple attempt to turn back is fraught with alternative action, because now 'it all looked different'.

Only an Easy Walk

The man set himself a 10-mile walk on the Pennines; nothing remote or difficult because he was out of training, but sufficient as a challenge. When he had done it he knew that he would feel satisfaction, and that he still had something of youth on his side. Knowing about the hills he was well prepared with good boots,

a lightweight rucksack and waterproof clothing, food, drink, first-aid kit, map, compass, torch with spare batteries, whistle, and even spare bootlaces. He showed his wife the roundabout route he intended to take from Edale to Kinder Downfall and back to Edale. She commented that if he did not phone her from Edale by 19.00 hrs she would contact the mountain rescue team.

It was a beautifully clear, though cool, May morning when he set off aiming to do the 10 miles in about 5 hrs, allowing for a pleasant pub stop. About three-quarters of a mile after starting his map showed the desired footpath; but the path itself was barred by a fierce notice saying No Footpath. The longer way round only added a little over a mile and the weather was fine; except that on looking around he saw that there was now more cloud than expected. He went on uphill towards the plateau, with a few home truths about his physical condition making themselves felt. His legs hurt already, his throat was dry, and his neck ached from looking up at the towering rocks. It was a steep climb up to those heights, made worse by a school party sprawled on the rim of the plateau with nothing to do but watch his progress. After a few stumbles he could not stand those critical eagle eyes any longer, so decided to avoid giving them any further free entertainment by setting off sideways around the hill. Out of sight, he would be able to retrieve his breath in peace. Finally he made the ridge and its plateau and opened a can of beer. Now the going should be easier. So far he had covered 2 miles in 3 hrs but drinking his beer in sweat-damp clothes he felt suddenly cold, and looked up to find the sun gone and the cloud thick. He took a compass bearing for his crossing of the plateau, but the going was not so easy; the plateau being of peat criss-crossed by gulleys, streams and banks. Finally he arrived at a path with people. Still feeling like an explorer after his rugged crossing he was startled to encounter a man with a woman who was dressed in high heels, pink coat and matching taffeta headscarf. The two smirked when they saw him which made him angry; people should not go into the hills in high heels. There was still more of the peat plateau to cross so he plodded on, until he realised that he did not know if the Kinder Downfall was now to the left or the right, because an insidious mist seemed to be obscuring anything distant. At this moment of doubt a group of three efficient-looking mountaineers appeared and went past him at a spanking pace, their equipment jangling. They even had a radio with a long floppy aerial. He wondered where they would be going to with such equipment, and with such determination and speed. Kinder Downfall, of course; where else? It all added up. Before they disappeared into the mist he took up a shadowing position 100 yds astern. He just managed to keep up without becoming too breathless, until about 15 min later when he woke up to the fact that wherever they were going, it was not Kinder Downfall. All this time he had been going in the opposite direction.

It was now four o'clock, the mist was thickening and the light was poor. The sensible thing would be to go home; but sense was defeated by ambition – to get to his goal. And after all, he did know where he was. He set off again, picking out and identifying landscape features, except that the distance to the Downfall seemed much greater than he had anticipated. Eventually he heard the rushing water before he saw it; but he had arrived. The route now was to go the short distance to Crowden Tower and then pick up the perimeter path to Grindslow; except that if he took a short cut across the peat on a compass bearing he would save time. About half-way across the morass and still staring at his compass he realised it was dark. The peat seemed to become rougher and it took a further 30 min to stumble across it. Then the expected gritstone boulders appeared. With relief he turned on to the path and walked on – to find a drop where there should not have been one. He returned to the gritstone boulders to have a think, and got out his torch. Thoughts of a possible cold night out started to bother him, so he decided to follow the path down regardless of where it went to; down was the way he wanted to go.

The decent was exhausting as his thigh muscles seemed to have seized up, and much of the path was only sheep track between rocks. After a while he paused and looked up at the black outline of the edge of the plateau above him, and recognised Crowden Tower. He was going the wrong way. He had to make a decision. He could either climb all the way back to the gritstone boulders and follow the path the other way to Grindslow and then on to Edale, or he could go on down the so-called path that he was on and hope to find the right path to lead him to Edale. It was his thigh muscles that made the decision; he continued on down. He did not find the right path. At one time he was knee-deep in swiftly running water. Later he picked his way, tottering between half a dozen little tents all glowing orange with warmth, but did not like to ask for directions.

At seven o'clock, and three wrong paths later, he was still far from Edale, but he knew that his wife would do as she had said and call out the rescue team. Seeing a cottage he knocked and asked to telephone. He knew the rest of the way home was now straightforward and easy so it seemed best to tell his wife he was at Edale, but saw the look of blank astonishment on the face of the telephone owner. At seven-fifteen he started off again, but the prospect of several miles of tarmac road was too much. There was a short cut; or rather several. He probably travelled them all. At eight o'clock he clambered over a style, fell in a ditch and just lay there. Then he staggered to his feet and stumbled across a hillside

until he came up against a barbed wire fence. Too exhausted to follow it to a gate he crawled underneath. Half-way and hooked up a torch was flashed in his face and a voice demanded to know where the hell he was going. 'Edale,' he muttered, and the voice relented and showed him how to do the last mile.

Although the first failure, that of the forbidden footpath, was not of his making, the inability to retrieve the situation reached almost classical proportions. But each error was an easy one to make.

Reading a Map

The ability to read a map or chart and extract from it *all* the information it can provide is fundamental for anyone going anywhere on their own. Yet it is a skill which many people neither develop nor practise. This is apparent with 'navigators' in a car. Even if there is every scale and type of map necessary to negotiate the road system there is a shattering difference in people's ability to assist the driver. Some drivers, faced with holiday traffic jams, can hand the passenger a 1-in. ordnance survey map and take to the lanes knowing that they will be promptly provided with all the information needed. Other passengers will have lost their drivers by the second crossroads.

Glider and balloon pilots do their navigation largely by map reading, and can become extremely good at it. Light aeroplane pilots used to have to develop the same skill, but now, with almost universal radio navigational aids, many do not do so. Some do not even carry a map. This is crazy; if the radio aids or even the electrics which power it go wrong the pilot is on his own, and this is not the time to learn how to read a map. Apart from being a basic skill, identifying the passing countryside is interesting, and often yields snippets of information of future usefulness, such as the location of a private landing strip as a possible bad-weather escape.

Maps and charts provide a mine of information which can be acquired through interpretation, or directly read. But they cannot supply answers if out of date, dog-eared on the folds – everyone knows that the most needed information is always on a fold – or covered with route lines. These should be in pencil, or in chinagraph on a plastic skin, and cleaned off before the next trip. Two very senior and experienced pilots flying a light aeroplane only just missed hitting a radio mast in thick weather because, although it was marked clearly on their aeronautical chart, they had obliterated the sign with a thick red crayon line for their route.

PART FOUR

◇ *After the Dust Settles*

An accident may happen with great suddenness, but it does not actually end until some sort of normal situation is restored. Regardless of whether it is a simple, and common, occurrence like falling down a cliff or more long term, like having the boat sunk by a whale in mid-Pacific, the ultimate severity of the accident may be in the hands of the victims themselves. It is a time for doing something.

The greatest block to immediate, sensible, and effective action is that the sudden change in circumstances brought about by the initial impact of the accident produces a traumatic and often paralysing sense of bewilderment: consider the solo pilot of a small single-engine aeroplane, ferrying it from the United States to South Africa. Now, this is quite a trip, and by the time the aeroplane had reached the Kalahari Desert it had covered many strange territories. It had also become home – comfortable and secure; camera and Polaroid specs, in their proper places, and everything organised. But flying had become boring, so to relieve the tedium the pilot flew low over the flat empty rippled sand of the desert – until a giraffe got up in front of him. When the dust settled he was just another feature in the hot wasteland, faced with a total change of life-style in 10 sec flat.

The resultant turmoil of thought should not be underestimated. For a start many people are unused to being on their own, let alone becoming instantly totally dependent upon themselves, so the first mental conflict is likely to be between an assumption that rescue will come, and a disorganised approach to doing something oneself – such as setting off for help with no plan at all. The conflict then easily develops into a hate against others 'all sitting comfortably' and doing nothing, and a growing panic about surviving at all. There are plenty of books showing how to build a still to obtain water, or an igloo for shelter, what fungus can be eaten, and how to survive in cold water, but none of this valuable information is of the least use unless the unhappy victim can get himself into the right attitude of mind *before* he starts making mistakes – or more mistakes. Some people are more philosophical than others, but the greatest safeguard is anticipation, in devoting thinking time ahead of any possibility of disaster as to how one would react. Such imaginative thinking should not, however, be limited to the more glamorous-seeming dramas of heroic crossings of the ice-cap or re-enacting Lindbergh; but about what is actually likely to happen to *you* when the boat engine won't start at the end of a day's fishing, or when hill-fog suddenly sweeps over the mountain when you are half-way along an unfamiliar short-cut late in the day. These, and falling off cliffs, are the sorts of accident that happen to *hundreds* of people in this country alone every year, and for which few are prepared – because they never expected it to happen to them.

The immediate follow-on from mental preparedness, even to some degree, is actual provision against emergencies; at the simplest end of the scale, having a plug spanner and spare plug for the outboard avoids the emergency all together. Almost certainly the most valuable aspect of sensible provision against emergencies is that it eases the much greater problem of mental gear-change. Knowing that you can continue to eat, or drink or have shelter, or light, or be able to attract attention reduces the corrosive feelings of helplessness and hopelessness.

On Your Own

Last year I was flying with a friend in a single-engine floatplane in the lake and forest country east of Lake Winnipeg in Canada. We were landing and taking off from water some 50 or so miles from the nearest person, let alone road or habitation. It only required a submerged log, engine failure, unexpected weather deterioration or any mistake by the pilot to produce a survival situation. The possibilities were real, but the homework had been done. Life-jackets were worn without question, an emergency bag and ELT (emergency location transmitter) were to hand in case the aeroplane sank totally; but if it did not, tucked in the back were sleeping bags, stove, a week's supply of dehydrated food – half the world's fresh water is readily available in Canada – axe, ropes, clothing, mosquito repellent and so on. We had absolutely no problem, only delightful flying, but being properly equipped engendered a good feeling of independence. Another pilot in Alaska was not so fortunate, and with a failing engine decided to make a precautionary landing on a large lake.

The water was glassy, making it impossible to assess height above it, so he made the standard type of power-on, nose-high approach for such conditions. But he got a little slow; and instinctively lowered the nose to gain speed, instead of increasing any power that was still available in his dying motor. At that instant he hit the invisible water surface, caught a float and turned over. Then all was quiet, and he climbed wet and suddenly cold on to the bottom of one of the floats – all that was left above the surface. He was $1\frac{1}{2}$ miles from shore and there was no wind at all to drift him anywhere. Swimming seemed impossible owing to the low water temperature, and the radio and ELT, both under water, were swamped and useless. Furthermore, he was not expected home for another 3 days. As evening arrived it became cold, a little above freezing, but the biggest problem was how to remain on the ridged and sloping top (bottom) of the float if he fell asleep. Remembering the nylon mooring cords on the tails of the floats, he collected them and tied himself on. Hope rose with the sunrise and a breeze started to blow him towards the shore: then it changed and drifted him away again. Then the aeroplane finally stopped on some underwater obstruction. Cold and stiff it was becoming increasingly difficult to stay on the float, but more alarming, there seemed to be less float to sit on. He scratched a mark at the water line and watched it very slowly submerge. There was no question now that the aeroplane was sinking, and there was no way of leaving it. He spent some time jotting down a letter to his wife, and a will, on a crumpled invoice found in his shirt pocket, and then tried to doze his way through a second cold night. The sun rose once more, and the scratched mark was an inch under water. In his enervated state he somehow had to make a plan to get ashore. He remembered several empty petrol cans inside the plane, enough to make a raft, but the thought of diving for them in the cold was inhibiting. After a while he took off his clothes, folded them carefully, and tied them to the float where they would keep dry. He knew the water would be cold, but the stabbing chill was numbing. Pushing off downwards, he found the aeroplane door open, but could not drag himself inside, and came up gasping for both air and warmth. For an hour he sat on the float shivering and hugging his clothes to him. It was not until the fourth attempt – each one requiring a fierce build-up of determination – and nearly 4 hrs later that he finally managed to push himself inside the door. In the murk he located the petrol cans floating up against the floor of the cabin. He grabbed a can and pushed off backwards. The can went faster to the surface hitting him in the face. Again he rested, dreading the prospects of getting the remaining cans, now his only chance of survival. But he got them one by one and tied them together with the laces from his boots. He was exhausted but realised that if he got ashore he would need his rifle, axe, and above all his glasses. His eighth freezing dive located the gun – through his feet – and also a sodden leather jacket. He got the axe on his ninth dive, but not his glasses. The tenth dive was a nightmare. He got the glasses, but for a while was too exhausted to climb back on the float. Eventually he did so, tied the last can to the other three, jammed the rifle barrel and the axe through the can handles, dressed slowly, and lying over the cans started to paddle towards the shore using his hands, and resting frequently. About 100 m from land he became entangled in water lily stalks.

He tried to part the lily pads with one hand and paddle with the other but he was now too exhausted to go on, and his legs sank down. In a daze he felt his feet touch bottom. He staggered to the shore, fell down to rest, and was set on by a cloud of devouring mosquitoes. With his face and hands rapidly swelling he started to cut spruce boughs to give him protection for the night, and shivering uncontrollably crawled under the branches. As sun rose on the fourth day, he saw that the floats had gone, and he knew he must make some sort of signal that could be seen by a passing aeroplane.

He cut down a 20-ft high spruce from the forest edge. It took time because he had now been without food for 4 days. He tied the four metal petrol cans to the top branches, dragged the tree to the water's edge, and somehow persuaded it to stand upright in the soft mud. There was nothing else he could now do, so he crawled under the spruce boughs and fell asleep.

Shortly afterwards a pilot on a fishing trip in his aeroplane happened to fly over the lake, and seeing some unusual glittering on the shore, went down to have a look. The pilot woke at the noise and staggered out, waving. An hour later an army helicopter arrived to take him home.

Resilience and the Right Attitude

The right mental attitude, and resilience, was demonstrated in the commonplace incident of being lost on the moors when a fifteen-year-old boy got caught out by mist, headed off on the wrong compass bearing, and became totally lost and disorientated. He stopped, and being equipped to look after himself the mental gymnastics needed to change gear were small. He knew the weather must clear in due time, and he knew that his friends would look for him. But four days later, when the mist eventually lifted, the rescuers knew they must be searching for a body. Instead, they found the boy in good health coming down to meet them. He had found a sheltered hollow, climbed into his sleeping bag encased in a large plastic bag, protected his primus from the rain and damp, and periodically brewed up some food. When the weather cleared he still had a reserve left from the three eggs, three packets of soup and a packet of orange drink.

Correct Decisions

In addition to the right attitude, correct decisions on priorities, and attention to physical protection, ingenuity moves rapidly up the scale as a valuable asset. Unusual situations demand original thought, a habit not often in demand. People are, in general, highly conditioned by what is normally done or expected, and have difficulty in changing to something less conventional, although more sensible. The aeroplane pilot with a failing engine may try to reach an airfield upwind, even though it is almost certain he will not make it, rather than to turn downwind towards open country where he will have more freedom of manoeuvre: people try to swim desperately to the nearest river bank where there are people instead of using the energy of the stream to land them on an empty shore a mile lower down.

One November day, at 11.40 one morning some 2 miles off the Cornish coast, a diver missed his cover boat, which was not where it should have been through engine failure. The boat skipper, having fixed his motor, later set off to search for the diver, failed to find him, and at 15.00 hrs alerted the coastguard who set in motion a shore and helicopter search. This latter was called off at 23.30, to be resumed at first light. At 03.00, 17 hrs after missing his boat, the diver walked ashore and found his own way to a near-by farmhouse. For all this time he had remained quite still floating in the water in his wet suit and conserving his energy and store of body warmth while the tide drifted him up the coast and back again. When it flooded for the second time he was near enough to land to be able to swim to the beach without becoming exhausted. Understanding the sea, he knew that by waiting it would work for him.

Ingenuity

In a self-help situation, knowing how to make use of natural energy and forces becomes important. For 5 days last year two men lived aboard an upturned trimaran in the Atlantic, resting in an upside-down bunk above water-level, and eating cold food. They were eventually spotted because they had smashed the boat's mirror and stuck bits at all angles over the surface of the hull bottom with epoxy to reflect the sun. A passing ship turned to investigate the odd glitter.

Some aspects of ingenuity need quick calculation – or be worked out in advance in a comfortable chair. Most sailing boats, for example, carry inflatable dinghies or liferafts, and the conventional idea is that when the boat is sinking the crew jump, with some provisions, into the inflatable and are saved. But if the skipper could calculate the buoyancy needed to keep his boat afloat, or had already done so, and if the leak could be controlled given time, it might be more sensible to inflate the dinghy or raft *inside* the boat, instead of outside. The calculations would obviously need to be right, but if so considerable drama could be averted.

Some years ago an MFV crew off Malta had difficulty raising the anchor, eventually discovering that they were also trying to haul up what looked like the Malta–Sicily telephone cable. Despite juggling with the capstan the cable could not be made to fall off the anchor flukes. It was two glider pilots on board who suggested tying the telephone cable to the MFV, lowering the anchor free, and then cutting the tie.

Three men wrecked their yacht on a Caribbean reef 15 miles from the nearest land. They lived on it for several days, while it pounded on the coral beneath them. But hoping to eventually save the yacht as well as themselves, they conserved their possessions and waited. Boats passed by, but no one saw them, and they had no more flares. Finally, the penny dropped. At regular short intervals they threw something that floated into the sea. After a while they had a pointer several miles long floating across the ocean, and within hours a fishing boat came motoring down the line. Although self-help in many situations involves rescue, many people are alive when the rescuers arrive because they have acted positively and relied on their own resources. This is a far removed situation from those who demand rescue to redeem their own incompetence or for convenience. One man on a boat *on moorings* fired a red flare for the lifeboat, because it was too rough for him to get ashore in his own dinghy!

Perhaps one of the more remarkable examples of self-reliance was the Alaskan pilot of a little, old, Piper Cub. He started the flight with two mistakes. He did not say where he was going; not so unusual for a pilot using his little aeroplane as many use their cars, and he left his main supply of survival rations behind; and who does not know the indecision problem with small craft of what to take and what to leave behind. Nevertheless, the mistakes were made. The afternoon was dying and the outside wing thermometer was showing 25° below, when he saw he had no oil pressure. Then the engine stopped. It was now dusk, with nothing but forest 1,000 ft below. Quietly the little Cub glided down, rustled into the gloom of the top branches, and with a scraping of timber, stopped. The pilot found he was quite unhurt. He got out, and discovered that apart from a bent propeller blade, and other minor damage, the aeroplane also seemed to be intact. The Cub still had its nose up some small trees, so he cut them down. The pilot knew where he was and being used to being in the woods on his own he made up a survival pack and set off to walk the 20 miles to the Yukon. After 3 miles in the snow, he realised he was making a disastrous mistake, and trudged back again. He then tried to work out why the engine had stopped and decided that the oil for some reason had congealed with cold. He cut down some timber to make a fire and a bed and then slept.

The next day he worked straightening the propeller, with a Spanish windlass made of young trees and nylon line. Eventually, he got it about right, and started on mending the rudder and re-attaching a ski. That night he cut down trees to clear a runway. By noon on the third day all was ready, although his right hand was now swollen and sore. He ate the last of his small supply of rations, warmed up his engine oil, paced the strip as 350 ft long, and reckoned that this was enough in the dense freezing air.

At 1,000 ft up he relaxed; and the engine stopped. Away to the left was a small frozen lake that he thought he could reach. He didn't, and once again listened to the familiar noise of splintering branches with a sinking heart. Again he was unhurt and climbed out. This time one undercarriage leg had been torn off, and there were more holes in the wings. The situation was now serious. Without a gun there was no food, and without food in the Alaskan winter he would soon die. There were about 150 trees between him and the lake. He started cutting them down. During the fourth day, he repaired the undercarriage by lashing on a wrench as a splint. He pushed the

Cub to the edge of the lake and winched it carefully down on to the ice with his nylon line. By the next midday he was ready to take off, but the sky was now overcast, and there were more flurries of snow. Several times he took off, but was forced back by the weather. Again he spent the night in his bed of branches.

At five o'clock the next morning he got up, lighted the catalytic heater under the engine to give a real warm-up to the oil, as the temperature in the night had subsided to 25° below. By 10.30 he was satisfied the engine would keep going, and took off. He climbed in the clear air to 4,500 ft to check his bearings, picked up a known river; and the engine stopped. This time he made a frozen lake in good order, sat on it for a while thoroughly warming the engine, and took off again. Fifteen minutes later a repeat performance had him landing on a frozen river. Off he went again, zigzagging between frozen lakes and clearings. Now he tried flying with the throttle wide open to try to keep the engine running less cold, and it seemed to work. Then he saw a village, and an airstrip. As he started down the engine stopped; but he made the strip. He had not used his ELT to summon help because he knew no one would search for him for several days more and he did not want to cause a bother.

Suddenly a Rescuer

Although sudden and extreme change of circumstances has its greatest impact on the victim, any person finding himself abruptly in the unexpected role of rescuer may be equally startled. Falling off a boat is a common occurrence, yet the cry 'Man overboard!' can temporarily stop logical thinking in its tracks. The problem is not only to find and get back to that small bobbing head, but often more difficult, to get a wet and heavy person aboard. Again, many excellent articles have been written on how to cope with the problem, all starting with the essential rule of having one person to watch the bobbing head *and do nothing else*. The training ship *Royalist*, crewed by young teenagers, has a no-messing approach of immediately putting a complete liferaft into the water, together with emergency gear, should a cadet go overboard. The swimmer – and he has to be able to swim – gets himself into the liferaft which is easy for him to see and waits to be picked up. Even if this takes some time, because of a raw crew or having to lower sail, the cadet is safe.

Amateur SAR

The most usual way of falling overboard is when sail changing on the foredeck, or being washed out of the cockpit by big waves, but avoidable in all but perhaps extreme storm conditions by sensible use of safety harness. In coastal and harbour sailing in reasonable weather a person going overboard is at least immediately seen, and often by other crews as well as his own. But it does sometimes happen on a long voyage that someone goes overboard for no apparent reason and this is not noticed for some time. The rescuer now has a real problem, with his thinking clouded by recrimination, or emotion if the crewman was a member of the family or close friend, as is likely to be the case. One morning a crew member of a yacht sailing downwind at 6 knots in the Atlantic trades woke early. It was a beautiful dawn, so he went on deck to chat with his friend on watch. The cockpit was empty. He looked over the empty foredeck in growing disbelief. He stared at the water astern, his heart beginning to thump loudly. He rushed down into the cabin, into the galley, the heads, the fo'c'sle. Nothing. He screamed 'Man overboard'. They were a competent crew, but it took the best part of half an hour to get down the twin foresails and all their gear, replace them with the main and working jib, and start back across the empty sea. But where exactly was back? No reciprocal compass heading, calculated reverse of the wind direction, or any other system or instinct could surely be accurate enough to find a tiny head in a huge ocean. And how far to go? The log had ceased to work, and in any case no one had the slightest idea at what time he had gone over the side. They thrashed that boat back against the trades in growing misery, with one crewman aloft, swaying precariously with binoculars. They changed tacks with measured timing and precision to keep as nearly as possible on an exact reciprocal course.

After 2 hrs in the water the crewman was chilled through and wondering idly about how long his body would take to sink to the bottom of the sea. He had come to terms with death, and was quietly looking at the sky and sea. Suddenly, he saw the tip of a white sail. His serenity departed. He screamed and waved and swore at his friends for being on a tack that took them away from him. He cursed them to hell. Then he saw the yacht come round towards him and the joy of living poured back. He could already feel himself being lifted out of the water by warm, strong arms. Then the yacht went about again, away from him. Suddenly delirious, he felt tormented, and hating his friends, he turned his back on the white sails and waited to die. But they had seen him and they picked him up. The cuts on his hands were from the thin log line that he had tried to hang on to, until it broke.

This rescue demanded not only competence of a high order, but clear thinking and calculation at a time of considerable emotional upset. It was a moment when no single error, however small, could be afforded. This is perhaps the essential point of any rescue activity. That the rescuer has not only to cope with the results of the mistakes of others, however valid their reason, but must avoid making any himself. He has to possess a sort of double competence. There is a natural and instinctive feeling deep in most people to aid their fellows in distress, but when this instinct takes over without organised thought or the skills to support it, there can easily be two tragedies instead of one. Disaster all too frequently follows where a child falls into a river, or bathes in rough waves. A passer-by dives in, clothed, mentally and physically unprepared, and drowns. The victim escapes more often than the rescuer.

Situation in Control

The quality probably most needed in the person who unexpectedly finds himself in the role of the rescuer, is the ability to maintain control over the unfamiliar situation with which he is confronted. This needs great awareness of what can still go wrong, and very clear thinking. Visualise the problem of suddenly finding yourself the only person around to rescue a sinking boatload of people, when all you have is a 9-ft inflatable with small plastic oars. Add to this the fact that you are only fourteen, had the boat for a recent birthday present, and are under parental instructions not to go out to sea. Just this happened to a Scout who was practising on the edge of the water, when he saw a speedboat stop about half a mile off the beach. A few minutes later he saw the occupants waving a white shirt. He looked around, but there were no other boats about, so he rowed out as fast as he could. The speedboat had had engine failure at speed, and the following wake had swept in over the transom. In spite of frantic bailing, they were now sinking. For the Scout there were rocks, and a 4–5 ft swell running which swirled the inflatable in the eddies, so it was a hard, long row. After some 20 min he neared the speedboat, and its owner swam to the inflatable. The boy continued to row, not

much helped by the man clinging on, and reached the sinking boat. In the water was another man wearing a life-jacket, an eight-year-old boy and a dog. He had just got the child and the dog into his inflatable when he saw a woman being dragged below the surface, snagged on the sinking boat. He caught hold of her by her long dress and held on while the owner clambered into the inflatable, and helped him pull her aboard. The remaining man with the life-jacket was now numb with cold, and unable to help himself. The Scout and the speedboat owner had a real job getting him into the now overcrowded inflatable, and when they finally got him aboard, he was unable to move. The Scout then began the long row back to the beach against the now ebbing tide. When he got his breath back, the owner of the speedboat took over one of the oars to help. It would have been easy for the inexperienced Scout to have failed to negotiate the rocks, to have lost his little oars when pulling people aboard, or to have had the dinghy unbalanced and upset by so many people. But he managed to avoid all of these pitfalls, and made no mistakes.

Quick Thinking Helps

Parachuting is a sport demanding particularly quick thinking if something goes wrong, particularly where beginners are involved. These normally carry out their first jumps attached to the aeroplane by a static line which automatically opens the parachute when it pulls taut. It is only rarely that the static line gets caught up, but when it does the new parachutist is left twirling around in the slipstream like a hooked and bewildered fish. Should this happen the parachutist in charge of the jumpers is in a dilemma, because he does not know if the beginner will now act correctly, or has become too confused or frightened to do so. To make sure, one instructor decided that he must make his way down the static line to the student. He and two others had already tried to pull the beginner back on board, but this had failed, so telling the pilot to gain height and return over the airfield, he asked one of the other parachutists to cut the line when he signalled. Overhanding down the line to the student he turned him so that the reserve chute on his chest would open without being obstructed by his body and signalled for the line to be cut. As the two of them fell away, the instructor pulled the beginner's chute, and as soon as he saw it open, let go of him. When they had separated enough he opened his own parachute, and they both landed on the airfield.

Not Always to Plan

But with the best will in the world, not all rescues go according to plan. Balloons, as everyone knows, only go downwind so it is quite a challenge to make a sea crossing, but balloonists are enterprising people and two of them decided to cross Brittany's Quiberon Bay, a distance of about 10 miles. The authorities laid down various stipulations and scheduled a police launch as escort, and a day eventually arrived with wind from the necessary SW direction, blowing with suitable gentleness. The balloon set off from the cliffs and floated over the clear calm sea, with the seabed visible, and pretty blue jellyfishes basking on the surface. Silently they drifted over a mass of sailing dinghies manoeuvring for a race start. They did not want to interrupt the concentration below, but a necessary blast on the balloon's burner produced astonishing disorder in the ranks. A few minutes later the wind just died; and by now they were into the third of their five propane cylinders. They descended to ask the police launch not to stray too far, and then went up to 1,000 ft to consider what was best to be done. The only possible answer seemed to be a tow from the police launch; this would be a new experience but one which might succeed. They descended to 150 ft and were about to dangle the trail rope to the launch when a helicopter arrived, and carefully tried to produce a local wind to ease the balloon towards land. Unfortunately, the turbulence was such that the balloon went flat and fell into the sea. In water up to mid-basket the crew full blasted the burner and, emerging like a sodden lobster pot, waved away the zealous helicopter. The guide rope, now heavy with water, halted the balloon at 150 ft. At this moment the police seized the guide rope end and set off full speed ahead, and once more the balloon went straight into the sea. Another full blast and again the balloon leapt from the water in dewy splendour. By now there was not much propane left, and it was essential to strike a compromise with their adversaries. They lowered themselves to about 10 ft, stabilised, and implored the police to *listen*. Following a speedily invented crash course on balloon towing, a settled situation was achieved with the basket about 8 ft above the water, and the boat motoring at 5–6 knots. Steadily, they approached the coast, and the balloonists were just congratulating themselves when, without any warning, the launch released the tow. Up shot the balloon, but with just enough impetus remaining to flop on to the dunes.

More Towing

Towing is a fairly ordinary rescue measure, from getting a car started, to helping a boat off a lee shore, but it is a practice little used except when something has already gone wrong; which is perhaps why much towing is unsuccessful. It is probably the glider-towing pilot who has more understanding of the art than almost anyone else, because he does it hundreds of times a year in all weathers. The usual towing mistakes are to underestimate the mass to be towed when starting off, to fail to appreciate the different behaviour of a vehicle when under tow, and to underestimate its ability to stop. But perhaps the most frustrating part of being towed, certainly in a glider, is when the tug pilot gets lost, and wanders off in what you know is the wrong direction. During gliding championships, some years back in South America, a pilot was being towed home at the end of a cross-country flight. He was tired, and longing to just get on the ground and have a long refreshing drink. He noticed the tug pilot was diverging from the correct track line, but visibility was good and he did not worry. He became somewhat more concerned when the destination airfield came abeam but some 10 miles away. He edged sideways on the tow to cause the tug pilot to look round, but he took no notice, or did not see his gesticulations in the cockpit. With a growing feeling of hopelessness mixed with irritation he sat at the end of the string, and tried to be patient. Sixty miles farther on the tug pilot ran out of petrol, and glided down to force-land in a field. Almost speechless with fury, the glider pilot released, marked the position on the map, found himself a thermal and laboriously soared 60 miles back home again. He felt better after telling the competition staff where they would find their tow pilot.

It would be quite wrong, although it may be understandable, if this book gave an impression that all amateurs are an accident-prone bunch of irresponsible idiots. The contrary is actually true, and the majority of people who sail, or whatever, are or become extremely competent. They are not much heard of because they do not get in the news. Everyone makes mistakes, from jumbo jet pilots downwards, but the good seaman or flier will quickly recognise his errors and retrieve the situation in time. This is why such people are good; not because they are faultless. Nevertheless, in spite of care in preparation and skill in the execution of whatever they are doing, people may from time to time be in such need of rescue. Yachts hit submerged obstructions – and such objects now include containers from ships – or are hit by whales. Aircraft have engine failure, divers are missed by their cover boats, mountaineers hit by rock falls, and potholers trapped by unforecast flash floods. Accidents that these people may be unfortunate enough to have are an integral part of the challenging activity to which they are devoted, and these risks are accepted.

Accidents which are not acceptable are those which occur quite unnecessarily, like the armadas of airbeds that drift out to sea in summer because parents fail to look after their children; or the pilot who spins in low-flying over his girlfriend's house. And closely associated with such idiocies are the calls for rescue services for people who motor to sea without a plug spanner, or wander into the hills without a map.

The problem for the 'professional' rescuer, of course, is that he is not in a position to choose. He has to answer every call because at the time he does not know whether it is frivolous or vital. And the risk for him may be even greater when the reason is trivial. It is as well that people who devote themselves to the rescue of others have such a deep sense of purpose.

Competence Plus

Of all people it is the rescuer who can least afford to make mistakes, not only because others are dependent on him, but because the conditions in which he starts his work may already have become marginal, if not severe. He has to be doubly competent. A lifeboatman must expect to spend 15 or 20 hrs out in a cold force 8, the helicopter pilot hover in half a gale with his rotor blades mere feet from a rock wall, or the coastguard go down a crumbling cliff alone on a dark wet night. No one in their senses would do these things, except to help their fellows.

Lifeboatmen also Swim

Classic pictures of lifeboats, for example, do little to indicate how often a crewman has to operate actually *in* the sea.

One occasion was on a cold February morning when a motor cruiser was reported as having turned upside-down in heavy seas near the harbour entrance. On arrival no survivors could be seen, but knowing the boat's layout, it was believed that its crew might be trapped in the wheelhouse and could be alive. One of the lifeboat's crew volunteered to swim on a line to the boat, to dive under and investigate, in spite of the force 5 wind and 12–14 ft swell. The crewman reached the motor cruiser and banged on the hull. No response. He then dived several times to see if he could find any sign of the crew, but it was difficult to see with the shallow water full of churned-up sand. He also could not swim underneath the boat because of its violent motion so near the bottom. He tried to attach a loop with his 2-in. polypropylene safety line, so that the motor cruiser could be towed, but the only place he could find was the bow pulpit. Gently the lifeboat started the tow with the crewman still in the water, but suddenly it was hit by a big sea, and the coxswain had to increase speed to keep control. This tore out the pulpit, and yanked the floating crewman through the water, fouling his line with the remains of the pulpit rail. The coxswain saw what had happened and stopped while the crewman freed himself. The lifeboat then took in the line and came round in deeper water to upwind of the upturned hull and floated a lifebelt down to the crewman. He swam for it, and after 13 min in the very cold sea was hauled aboard. The lifeboat stood off, the crew concluding that there was regrettably no chance of anyone being alive in the motor cruiser.

In recent years the R.N.L.I. have added I.L.B.s, powerful inflatables for shallow water work, to supplement the big lifeboats. One I.L.B. was called out by the coastguard to a small motor boat seen drifting close to rocks, in a force 6 onshore wind with a big swell.

The boat was located 150 yds from steep cliffs and breaking seas, but the owner had now managed to get his anchor to hold and was in no immediate danger. However the other two people on board had swum for the shore. One could be seen lying safely on the cliff top but the other was on a rock at the base of the cliff surrounded by heavy surf. The I.L.B. helmsman anchored and backed the I.L.B. towards the cliffs under power, and as they neared the rocks stopping and lifting the engine. Then they continued by rowing. On the first landing attempt, the boat was swept broadside on to a rock, and on the second it was completely overwhelmed by the sea, finishing up full of water on a rocky ledge, but close to the man. One of the crew scrambled over to get him back to the I.L.B., which was slowly emptying itself because of its steep angle on the ledge. Just as the man, who was in bad shape with cuts and bruises, was got aboard another sea swept the I.L.B. off the rocks, but leaving the crewman on them. He was washed off by the next wave, grabbed a line thrown to him and was hauled into the boat. The crew pulled themselves into deeper water along the anchor line so that the engine could be restarted.

It is not, of course, only problems of wind, waves and weather with which lifeboatmen have to contend. Two of them took an I.L.B. to pick up a couple of girls cut off by the tide, but their large alsatian refused to allow the men to take the girls on board. Ever patient, the lifeboatmen got into the water and held the boat against rocks so that the girls and the dog could get themselves into the boat. They did so, but then the alsatian, teeth bared, refused to allow the men back in; so they had no alternative but to swim home pushing the boat ahead of them.

Sometimes it is All Too Much

Sometimes the conditions under which a rescue is attempted are so difficult that it fails, regardless of the determination displayed in carrying it out, and one of the problems that turns up frequently – and is very understandable – is that the master or owner of a vessel does not want to leave his ship. Somehow, he believes or hopes that it can be saved, and this belief is held often too long after the situation is even remotely retrievable. This happened on a small fishing boat which made a distress call and was rolling in big waves. A helicopter arrived and managed, in spite of the gyrating mast, to lift off a fifteen-year-old crew member. The winchman then returned for the other two crew, but they did not want to leave, so he detached himself from the winch cable to try to persuade them. At this moment the boat rolled ever more wildly and the dangling winch hook caught in the rigging. So as not to endanger the helicopter he signalled for the wire to be cut, stranding him, and the chopper returned to base. Shortly afterwards it was replaced by a second helicopter. In worsening weather, its winchman was now lowered but still the two fishermen refused to leave, so the two winchmen decided to return to the helicopter in a double lift. The cable was let out to maximum length to keep the helicopter wheels clear of the tossing mast, but as the two winchmen started to go up, the cable tangled with the radio aerials, which did not break. The crew in the helicopter had no alternative but again to cut the winch cable. The two men fell heavily on the boat rail and then into the sea. The original winchman bruised his arm, but the second broke his ribs and was knocked out. The first managed to get out of the strop, free himself from the hook and 60 ft of cable, and inflate his life-jacket. He held on to the unconscious winchman, and gave him mouth-to-mouth resuscitation while getting him to the fishing boat. Aboard, he continued, although exhausted, to give first aid, until a rescue boat arrived and took off all four from the foundering trawler.

Learning about Risk

The person whose job it is to rescue is no superman, but much the same as everyone else. It is not just the extensive and exhaustive training of a helicopter pilot that keeps him out of difficulties – all pilots, regardless of their training, make mistakes. It is because the rescuer has to operate constantly confronted with real danger that makes his senses and skills sharp. He has a deep appreciation that a mistake is a luxury that cannot be afforded. He also learns humility, because he knows how easy it would be for the boat pounding itself to pieces on the rocks to be his, and how easy it is to slip on the cliffs. He has developed an awareness; that mixture of unconscious, but continuous, observation and assessment of what is going on around him.

But the most important of all these is the nearness of danger, learning how to deal with it, and not be defeated. The rescuer has to put himself at risk, and by doing so learns how to be safe.

One fundamental problem with using the air or the sea for fun, or even serious pleasure, is that it is supposed to be done safely according to the rules. People are expected not to have accidents and are blamed if they do, and yet the best teacher of all – the facing of real danger – is as far as possible removed from them. Rules and regulations have this as the first priority. Training courses are organised to give pleasure and confidence, brochures add pictures of warm summer days, equipment is styled to be attractive to the eye. There is nothing wrong with this, except for the information which is left out – that it is all bloody dangerous if you do not do it right.

The other problem is that people tend to learn in detail about whatever it is they like doing best, and ignore other, wider skills or knowledge. They become specialists. But in reality only a relatively small part of flying or diving is specialised; the rest is common sense, and the reassembling of existing knowledge and experience. Accidents happen without warning and need correct remedial action fast. But often the best remedy comes from common sense and quick thinking, and not from a specialist approach.

A few years ago four people were sailing along in a well-found 35-ft motor sailer in a brisk force 5–6 breeze. No one was wearing a life-jacket because there was no need, and the skipper and his mate were good, experienced sailors. Then suddenly, at the same moment as the boat gybed unexpectedly, the mate stood up. He was knocked overboard, stunned. The skipper now had an urgent problem of what to do. He was a strong swimmer, and could save his friend, but the other two people aboard did not know how to handle the boat, and he could not send them, indifferent swimmers, into the water. As quickly as he could he lowered the jib, started the engine and returned to his mate who still gave some appearance of being alive. So the owner went in after him and got him alongside the boat. He called to the two on board to give him a loop of rope so that he could get himself and the mate back on to the boat but they were not able to do anything to help. They were bewildered, frightened, and unused to coping with real danger at first hand, and on their own. It is pointless to analyse such a disaster. Mistakes were made, as will happen, but no one was capable of retrieving the situation.

There is little doubt that the biggest cause of accidents is through people getting themselves into situations for which their experience is inadequate. Whether by this time the first mistake has or has not already been made is immaterial, because they will then make more. And most of these mistakes will be because they have no real understanding of the problem and are not capable of assessing the risk. But it has to be appreciated that many of the things that people, with any enterprise at all, want to do with their time are of an exploratory nature; technical, environmental, or simply to find out about themselves. By the very nature of such activities mistakes will inevitably be made, and some people will become killed.

It is unrealistic, and also quite wrong, to attempt to 'prevent' accidents. Regulation is a blunt weapon which can restrict and limit the learning process, or in the ultimate engender a disregard for rules. Overprotection produces people unable to properly act on their own initiative, and who have a negligible comprehension of risk. It has to be accepted that any venture containing challenge also contains risk, and it has to be accepted that people want to do challenging things; because they have a fundamental need to find out and explore. But although a lot of humans do stupid things they do like to stay alive, and do, in fact, themselves exert quite a strong regulatory effect on accidents.

If among aerobatic pilots, or divers, for example, the fatality rate is considered to be going above what they themselves feel to be acceptable, action will be taken to restore the *status quo* of acceptability. If accident *rates* for various established sports are studied it will be found that they remain surprisingly constant overall. Every few years they will peak up for some reason such as complacency, worse than average weather, or some new technical factor, and then subside to normal. The rate for each activity will be different because the basic risks are different, but since the people involved do it because they want to, they accept those risks.

Light aeroplane flying, for example, has a rate very slightly higher than scuba diving, which is in turn slightly higher than gliding. But all these rates of around 30–40 fatalities per 100,000 participants per year are acceptable, and are appreciably lower than some heavy industries, which are around 60. Sailing, on the other hand, is way down, less than four, though the rate for motor boats is a little higher. It is, of course, not possible to obtain either really accurate or fair comparative figures; the point is that if people find their friends and fellows being knocked off at an unacceptable rate to them they either go home – and the activity declines – or take action to stop the rot.

During the Second World War it seemed that a casualty rate of 20 per cent (per year, per operational tour, or equivalent effective period) was a critical point of acceptability; better than 20 per cent, or having a four-out-of-five chance of staying alive, and no one got too bothered about the risk to themselves. Worse than this and death seemed depressingly imminent. Operational considerations were, of course, also adversely affected due to constant changes in personnel.

What is Acceptable?

For recreational activities, when people are not expecting to be shot at, the acceptable rate is naturally very different. If it stays at 1 in 2,000 or better the accident has a remoteness and is definitely in the 'won't happen to me' range. But if or when the rate approaches 1 fatality per 1,000 participants the situation changes markedly in a number of ways: the likelihood of having an accident is seen to be too close to home – it *could* happen to me; there is an increase in adverse publicity and public disapproval; outside authority becomes concerned, bringing the threat of regulation; insurance rates increase; and pressure to give up the activity is applied by family and friends.

Because people enjoy their chosen sport, do not wish to give it up, and do not relish ideas of outside interference, the result of these pressures and changes in attitude is a closing of ranks, and action. National associations, journals, and clubs all concern themselves with analysing the problems. New standards and modified training schedules are introduced, and educational programmes and articles produced until the rate moves back into the acceptability range.

The most likely occasions for sports to approach the red line is during their formative years, or following an unexpectedly sudden increase in popularity. In its early days in this country sport parachuting went through a period when the fatality rate became unacceptably high to the people involved, and was corrected by a strenuous remedial programme set up by the British Parachuting Association. Hang gliding is currently in the same development problem stage, and the British Hang Gliding Association is equally engaged in a similar positive exercise. In the 1960s the affluent society vastly and rapidly increased the boat owner population. With no single organisation at the time to deal with an increasingly serious situation, responsibility was shouldered by the sailing magazines who all, at different levels, embarked on an extensive and effective campaign of educational articles; which still continues. The threat to boating's freedom from regulation was also reduced by the reorganisation of the old Yacht Racing Association to become the Royal Yachting Association.

This self-regulatory process is effective, because it stems from the need by the people concerned to keep the risk to themselves at an acceptable level. In no recreational sport, of the sort that this book is about, has the accident rate got out of hand. If external regulation is applied, before the rate reaches the limit of acceptability to the people involved, a few lives may be saved in the short term, but the real risk level will be less well learnt and appreciated. As a result the internal intent and energy to raise standards, improve training, and otherwise deal with the problems will be less. The most powerful remedial force is when people realise that they themselves could get killed quite easily. If this is not accepted, and people are prevented from doing the things they like doing, even if some of the time they do not do them very well, then frustration becomes a major factor in the way people live their lives. In the long run the overall accident rate, from all causes, will worsen.

In the end it comes back to the individual. He has to teach himself to rely upon himself, and learn how to cope with potentially dangerous situations without getting killed in the process. He has to develop his skills and broaden his own experience, but at a rate that he can manage. This is a difficult path to tread, but there is no other way. Of course lessons should be taken, books read, friends talked to, and rules remembered, but none of these things are of much value if the individual himself cannot learn to control his own destiny.

◇ INDEX

accident proneness, 47–8

accidents, continuous process, ix; effects of over-regulation, xi, 232; understanding causes, xi; forgetfulness, 4–5; irresponsibility, 9–10; fuel problems and failure, 12, 41, 42, 100; build-up of errors, 13–24, 50, 51–2; get-home-itis, 25, 36–8; compared with bad luck, 48; lack of judgement, 51; avoidance through good teaching, 54; communication failure, 64, 73–4; location of victims, 76–8; avoidance through anticipation and observation, 81–4, 88–9, 90–2; use of ingenuity, 86–7, 214–17; part played by equipment, 97, 102–3, 133; misuse of controls, 105; impact speeds, 117; survival aids, 117–18; propellers, 135–8; contributory factors, 141–53; weather-related, 173, 175–8, 180–3; self-help, 209, 210, 211–13; traumatic effect, 209–10, 229; lack of experience, 230; acceptability range, 230–2; occurrence in formative years, 232

adjustable buoyancy life-jackets (A.B.L.J.s), 51, 54, 104, 107–8, 148

aerobatics, emergency, 26–9

aeroplanes, sophisticated equipment, ix, 4; take-off errors, 11–12; misjudgements in fuel supply, 12, 41, 42, 100, 195; fuel systems, 100–2; engine failure, 101; inadequacies in equipment, 102–4; static generation during refuelling, 168; weather needs, 175; altimeters, 185

air, 50; nitrogen content, 145; the bends, 145; see also hypoxia

air pressure, altitude changes, 142–3, 185

Air Traffic Control, 21, 79

air transport hazard, reporting, 80

aircraft, 26; in hostile element, 33; instrument panels, 118–19; weight factor, 126; propeller accidents, 134–6; lightning risks, 171; airframe icing, 189–90; ice on take-off, 190

alcohol, effect of, 151–3

anchor-chains, accidents, 133

anticipation, 'visualising the scene', 18, 21, 88, 90; and avoiding disaster, 82–3; homework, 90–1, 212; thinking ahead, 210

apprehension, 25

Australia, survival situations, 13, 18–20

balloons, ballooning, xii, 221–2; accidents, 5–6; hot-air, 35, 104, 167, 168, 175; maintenance, 123; explosions in hydrogen-filled, 167–8, 171; weather needs, 175; navigation by map, 205

bathing fatalities, 9

bends, the, 145

boats, maintenance responsibility, 123, 126; collisions due to drift, 158; explosions, 165, 166; lightning strikes, 171; going aground, 194, 199–200; getting lost, 194–200; see also sailing; small boats

British Hang Gliding Association, 232

British Parachuting Association, 232

buoyancy aids, 107; wet suits, 110–11, 116; see also life-jackets

canoeing, white water and surf, 35; lucky escape, 46–7; maintenance of glass-fibre, 126

capsize drill, 60

carbon monoxide poisoning, 148–9